THE SINKING OF THE LANCASTRIA

THE SINKING OF
— THE —
LANCASTRIA

THE TWENTIETH CENTURY'S DEADLIEST NAVAL
DISASTER AND HOW CHRCHILL MADE IT DISAPPEAR

JONATHAN FENBY

CARROLL & GRAF PUBLISHERS
NEW YORK

THE SINKING OF THE LANCASTRIA

Carroll & Graf Publishers
An Imprint of Avalon Publishing Group Inc.
245 West 17th Street
11th Floor
New York, NY 10011

AVALON
publishing group incorporated

Library of Congress Cataloging-in-Publication Data is available.

ISBN: 0-7867-1532-4

9 8 7 6 5 4 3 2 1

Printed in the United States of America
Distributed by Publishers Group West

To the memory of those who died
on the Lancastria – and to those
who survived

CONTENTS

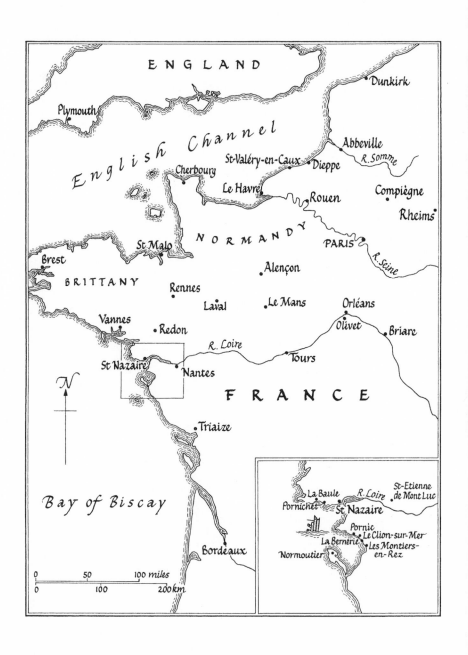

ENGLAND

Plymouth

English Channel

Dunkirk

Abbeville

St-Valéry-en-Caux

Dieppe

R. Somme

Cherbourg

Le Havre

Compiègne

Rouen

Rheims

St Malo

NORMANDY

PARIS

R. Seine

Brest

BRITTANY

Alençon

Rennes

Laval

Le Mans

Orléans

Vannes

Redon

Olivet

Briare

R. Loire

St Nazaire

Nantes

Tours

FRANCE

N

Triaize

Bay of Biscay

Bordeaux

| 0 | 50 | 100 miles |
| 0 | 100 | 200km |

La Baule

R. Loire

St-Etienne de Mont Luc

Pornichet

St Nazaire

Pornic

Le Clion-sur-Mer

La Bernerie

Les Montiers-en-Rez

Normoutier

ACKNOWLEDGEMENTS

I WAS FIRST TOLD about the *Lancastria* by Tom Wallace, and so owe a prime debt to him and his wife for having put me on the trail that led to this book. It could not have been written without the help of the Lancastria Association, and its compilations of recollections of survivors edited by John L. West and Colin Clarke in 1988 and 1998. I am deeply grateful to the Association for its help, particularly to the Secretary, Rob Miller. Equal thanks goes to survivors for their memories, papers and photographs, in particular to Fred Coe, Stan and Vic Flowers, Harry Harding, Denis Holland, Morris Lashbrook and Joe Sweeney. Another major source was the thirty hours of oral history from survivors recorded by the Imperial War Museum whose staff was especially helpful. I am also grateful for help from the Public Records Office at Kew, Steven Prince of the Naval Historical Branch of the Ministry of Defence, and Allen Packwood of the Churchill Archive at Cambridge.

Warrant Officer David Curry provided material on RAF units involved in the disaster, as well as showing me objects from the *Lancastria* collected at RAF Digby and letting me read his own work on Operation Aerial. I drew on Harry Grattidge's memoirs and on Cunard accounts of the liner's peacetime career. Hugh Stephenson provided unpublished extracts from Barry Steven's diary to throw light on the decision not to leave St-Nazaire. John Duggan recounted his family's exodus and read the manuscript. Jack Altman provided a lead that helped to get the project going. Sally Tagholm provided valuable help with the research and Sara Arguden gave her usual aid and comfort.

In France, Christophe François was an invaluable guide and an unselfish provider of material. I was also grateful for the assistance of Claude Gurio, Emile Bouton, the inhabitants of Les Moutiers, Thérèse Dumont at the Mayor's office in St-Nazaire, Yannick Bigaud, Mayor of Guémené-Penfao, and Dr Tessier of St-Nazaire. The Naval Archive at Vincennes. The departmental archives at Nantes and the Eco-Musée at St-Nazaire both provided local material including Denise Petit's account.

André Villeneuve gave useful books and thoughts on the collapse of France, and he and his wife, Lisa, were generous hosts during research in Paris. Annie and the late Luc Besnier supplied a most agreeable haven on trips along the Loire.

Christopher Sinclair-Stevenson was his usual supportive self. Andrew Gordon's encouragement fuelled the writing, and he nudged me to give the story a proper ending. Cassandra Campbell was an ideal editor, and the manuscript benefited from the attentions of Carol Anderson and Samantha Bell.

As always, I am hugely indebted to my wife, in the research in France, in improving the manuscript in many ways, and in her enthusiasm for telling the story of the *Lancastria*.

THE SINKING OF THE LANCASTRIA

PROLOGUE

'THIS IS THE END,' thought Captain Field, lying on his back in the oily sea. 'What a place to drown.'

Around him, the sea was covered with the dead and dying. Desperate people were fighting for their lives, grasping hold of planks, chairs, military packs, oars – or one another – as they battled to stay afloat. Behind them, silhouetted against the sky, a throng of soldiers crowded on the upended hull of the great ship which was sinking deeper in the water by the minute. Raging fires inside the hold sent up huge palls of smoke.

A few hours earlier, thousands of soldiers and air crew who had boarded the ship had regarded her as their escape route to England, and safety. They were among the forgotten men of the early summer of 1940.

After the Dunkirk evacuation ended at the beginning of June, Winston Churchill had assured the nation that 'the

British Expeditionary Force has been completely and successfully evacuated from France'. That was a spectacular piece of disinformation. Around 150,000 British troops were left behind, strung out from Champagne to the west coast.

Some trailed across France for two weeks as the German army advanced remorselessly and dive bombers swooped from the clear summer skies. Others stayed put in their bases in the west of France before finally being given the order to head to the coast for evacuation home.

Reaching the last open harbour at St-Nazaire, they had seen the five-decked, 16,243-ton *Lancastria* lying out in the wide estuary of the River Loire. She was the largest of a fleet sent to save tens of thousands of men crowding into the port town. As they swarmed aboard the former Cunard liner turned into a troopship, some felt it was almost as good as being back in Blighty. One thought the ship looked as solid as the Strand Palace Hotel in London.

In the mid-afternoon of 17 June, four bombs from a German plane hit the *Lancastria,* causing her to list sharply and then to turn over in the water.

For those caught in her holds when the bombs exploded inside the ship, she became a death trap of destruction and raging flames. Eight hundred RAF men died when a bomb hit the hold where they were sheltering. Another ripped through the ship's hospital. Steam escaping from a ruptured boiler horribly scalded stokers.

For others, the sinking hull of the overturned liner became the last place of refuge. At first, they screamed and shouted at the planes swooping down to machine-gun the wide bay. Some called for an RAF ace, 'Cobber' Kain, who had shot down seventeen enemy aircraft – not knowing that he had been killed in an accident two weeks earlier. Then they began to sing; first, the pub favourite, 'Roll Out the Barrel', and, led by a strong tenor voice, 'There'll Always Be an England'. An immaculately turned-out officer standing on the sinking keel smoked a cigarette as if he was safe on dry land. Looking back while he swam away, a 19-year-old Welsh trooper, Henry Harding, saw figures trying to scramble out of the portholes as flames flared in the hull. He could glimpse hands behind the bodies, either trying to push them out or pull them back. 'If there's a Hell, that's it,' he said to himself.

For those who jumped into the sea, the priority was to get away before the suction of the fast-sinking vessel dragged them down. Many ripped off their clothes to ease their progress through the water as oil spewed from the ship's ruptured tanks. Captain Field decided it was time to remove his trousers to make swimming simpler.

Another officer, Captain F. E. Griggs of the Royal Engineers, was moving as fast as he could through the warm, calm water. The previous week, he had been enjoying French food and wine as he drove across the country. Now, he was swimming for his life. Unlike many of those around him, he retained his full uniform with its Sam Browne belt, shoes, tin hat, plus a life belt. Oil coated him from head to foot. A German plane came over to strafe, but its machine-gun bullets missed him. The surface of the sea around him was strewn with dead small fish. 'I've got the oil and the sardines,' Griggs thought. 'All I want now is the tins!'

After jumping from the ship, Sergeant Harold Pettit had dropped deep below the surface, and felt he was bound to drown. Then he had come up, but he was suffering from sickness and diarrhoea. He joined a circle of five men, a couple of whom had life jackets. The six of them clung together, occasionally losing their grip because of the slimy oil and their tiredness, though they still had enough spirit to joke about their appearance. Weakening, Pettit thought he was going to go under again. Then, he suddenly heard a voice saying, 'Don't go yet, there's annuvver one 'ere' – and he was hauled, naked and covered with oil, on to a raft towed by a launch from a British destroyer.

Sidney Dunmall, a private in the Pay Corps who had been among the last to board the *Lancastria*, dug his nails into a plank thrown down from the ship, hanging on desperately as he tried to get away. But the suction dragged him back, and his plank banged against the side of the liner. Just then, a man wearing a life jacket swam by.

'I'll pull you clear, matey, if you promise not to hold on to me,' he called out.

'I won't touch you,' Dunmall replied. 'Just pull me clear.'

The man got on top of one end of the plank, and manoeuvred it fifty yards from the hull.

'Are you all right, matey?' he asked.

Dunmall thanked him. The man waved, and swam away.

A soldier without a life jacket approached an RAF man, who was wearing one, and said very politely: 'Good afternoon. I propose to share your life jacket.' The RAF man, Sergeant Macpherson, took it off, and they used it as a buoy, sculling with their spare arms to move away from the ship.

Some of those in the water went mad, ranting and raving. Others were silent in prayer. Many were choking on the 1400 tons of oil that poured out of the liner's tanks.

'My baby, look after my baby,' a woman shouted.

'It's all right ma, we've got her,' came a call, and men swam up holding the child above the water.

'Baby, baby,' the mother said repeatedly as she headed with her 2-year-old daughter for a raft.

One of the oldest soldiers on board, a 64-year-old Boer War veteran called Norman de Coudray Tronson, had helped to fire a Bren gun at the attacking planes; but then a wave washed him overboard, and he floated in the sea, looking back at the liner.

Captain Clement Stott had gone under the water after jumping from the ship, having carefully arranged his pince-nez in his breast pocket before launching himself into the air. As he came up, he felt a man hanging on to his feet. Stott realised he had to get rid of him, or they would both drown. So he kicked hard with his army boots, and struggled free.

A 44-year-old father of five from Wales who had brought his fifty men of the Pay Corps safely to St-Nazaire, Stott watched a naked man wearing a green and red identity disc round his neck dive through a porthole into the sea. At first, Stott could not spot anybody alive in the mass of wreckage and burned and blackened bodies, and already counted himself among the dead. But then he noticed a crowd of people, including some men from his unit, and raised his thumb in greeting. As he trod water, he saw they were all pitch black. 'That's a funny thing,' he thought. 'I didn't see any Africans aboard.' Then he became aware of the oil spread over the surface of the sea – his own face was also completely black.

Stott swam towards a raft crowded with men singing 'Roll Out the Barrel'. But a voice shouted 'Get off! Get away!', and feet in grey army socks kicked him in the face – Stott, 5 feet 5 inches tall and of slight build, was glad that, unlike him, they had taken off their boots.

In places, the thick oil slick caught fire from the German strafing. When a blazing patch threatened a lifeboat, a sailor jumped over the side to try to put it out; as he hit the water, he cried out, and was seen no more.

William Knight, who had fought his way across France after Dunkirk, saw a man swimming past a flaming patch of oil towards the float on which he sat. Suddenly, the man's hair caught fire. He began to scream. His head went under, and the oil closed over him.

Two soldiers shot one another to avoid drowning. A man was stuck in a porthole, the equipment he wore trapping him; somebody bashed him over the head with a piece of wood to save him from a lingering death as the side of the ship came down to the level of the sea. People who could swim or had life belts found themselves dragged down by those who could not or did not. A 13-year-old girl refugee dropped from the ship to the sea holding her father's arm; on the way down, she lost her grip and fell alone – she never saw him again. A lifeboat full of people plunged vertically into the water after somebody mistakenly cut its rope. An officer from the liner tried to help a man by pulling him along by his hair: it took him some time to realise that all he had in his hand was a severed head.

Circling the stricken *Lancastria* in his Hurricane, which had been sent to help defend the evacuation fleet from German planes, Norman Hancock brought his fighter low over the ship, and threw his Mae West life jacket down from the cockpit. People below cheered. Then, his fuel running low, Hancock turned and headed back to the airfield at Nantes.

Sitting on a hatch cover, Donald Draycott, an RAF ground crewman from Derbyshire, was surprised at how calm he felt. A travelling salesman for a tobacco company before joining the air force, he had been one of the first to jump from the ship. As he looked back at the 16,000-ton liner with her grand sweeping decks, Draycott thought: 'You'll never see anything like this again.' He watched people throwing life jackets through portholes and diving after them, only to find that those already in the water had grabbed them. He heard 'Roll Out the Barrel' 'as though it had been sung in an English pub'.

Twenty minutes after the German dive bomber had swooped out of the sky, the *Lancastria*'s upturned hull came level with the water. Men on the keel were still singing 'There'll Always Be an England'. Enemy fighters came in low, machine-gunning. Then the ship went under.

News of the disaster reached London as Winston Churchill was sitting in the Cabinet Office looking out at Whitehall bathed in early summer sunshine. He decided that there had been quite enough bad war news for a single day. France was suing for peace with Germany. Hitler and Mussolini were holding a triumphal meeting in Munich. Invasion forces were massing on the other side of the Channel; and the Luftwaffe was about to launch massive bombing raids on British cities. So the Prime Minister ordered that the sinking of the *Lancastria* was not to be reported in the media for the time being. In the rush of events, as he put it, he forgot to lift the ban.[1]

Survivors returning to ports in southern England in the following days were told not to talk about their experience. In any case, many of them preferred to try to forget. Giving his recollections more than half a century later, one soldier who supported himself in the water by stretching his arms across corpses wearing life belts, said he had not spoken before to anybody about the disaster, not even to his wife or two sons, because 'it is still a painful memory'.

The news was published in a newspaper in New York nearly six weeks later, with photographs taken by a sailor who had been on a destroyer in the rescue fleet. As a result, it surfaced in the British press, but only for one day's editions. After that, the tragedy vanished from public view, becoming a footnote to the history of the Second World War. There would be other, more glorious, events to savour – the Battle of Britain, El Alamein, the invasion of Italy, D-Day and the final defeat of Hitler. Though associations of survivors fought to keep alive the memory of what had happened off the coast of France on 17 June 1940, the sinking of the *Lancastria* disappeared into national amnesia.

The torpedoing of the liner, the *Lusitania*, in the First World War is well known. The death toll was 1195. The sinking of the *Titanic* is even more familiar, with its 1522 fatalities. On the lowest count, the death toll when the *Lancastria* went down off St-Nazaire was well above that of those two other disasters combined.

In his war memoirs, Churchill put the loss at 'upwards of 3000 men'.[2] Crew members were recorded as saying that the number on board was more than 6000. Some estimates have put it considerably higher. Survivors numbered around 2500. So, at its lowest, the death toll appears to have been in excess of the number Churchill mentioned – at least 3500 or 4000.

The sinking of the *Lancastria* certainly brought the greatest loss of life in any single British maritime disaster. But those who died that June afternoon have been forgotten except by the survivors and families who gather once a year at a church in London to remember them, and to give thanks for their own survival. This book tells their story, and the story of how they found themselves on the *Lancastria* that summer day and how they fought for their lives in oily waters among thousands of dead and dying.

CHAPTER 1

Friday, 14 June 1940

IT WAS, THE CHIEF OFFICER of the *Lancastria* decided, time to buy himself a good meal. Harry Grattidge and the rest of the crew had been at sea for much of the ten months since the outbreak of war with Germany. Gone were the days of cruising to the Norwegian fjords, the Mediterranean and the West Indies, of five-course dinners and of days filled with shore visits, bridge and whist drives, lotto parties, treasure hunts, concerts and, during a stopover in Cadiz, a cricket match at which gentlemen passengers beat the ladies by 107 runs to 85.

When war was declared in September 1939, the *Lancastria* had been on a cruise to the Bahamas. Her captain was told to head immediately for New York. When she sailed from Nassau, a crowd of local inhabitants turned out to see her off, but there was no cheering, and the ship left in the most profound silence Harry Grattidge had ever heard. 'All of us sensed that it would never be the same again,' he recalled.[1]

In New York, the liner was fitted out as a troopship. Non-essential crew were disembarked, including the musicians who played beside the sprung dance floor and the gardeners who tended the plants in the verandah café and the potted trees on the promenade deck. The gleaming hull and superstructure in the black and white livery of the Cunard Line was painted battleship grey. So was the single red funnel topped by a black band. The portholes were blacked out. A 4-inch gun was fitted as her sole armament. Then she sailed back to her home port of Liverpool without an escort.

In the following months, the *Lancastria* crisscrossed the Atlantic, ferrying men and supplies to and from Canada. In the late spring of 1940, she joined a convoy of twenty ships evacuating Allied troops from the ill-judged campaign to halt the Nazi advance in Norway. On the way back, the *Lancastria* was the target of an air attack, but the bombs fell wide. After disembarking the dirty, depressed troops in Scotland, it was time for another trip north, this time with men to garrison Iceland.

Returning from that voyage, the *Lancastria* called at Glasgow, where her captain asked for surplus oil in her tanks to be taken off, but there had not been time to do so before she sailed on to Liverpool. Knowing of the high losses of merchant shipping, including the Cunard liner, the *Carinthia*, which had been sunk by a German submarine the previous month, the crew were tense. They had spent months on repeated voyages without any proper defence against German planes and submarines. But now, there was the promise of a rest while their ship was reconditioned in her home port.

As soon as the *Lancastria* berthed in the Mersey, her captain, Rudolph Sharp, went ashore, crossing the broad river to his home in Birkenhead. Harry Grattidge called the 330-strong crew together in the dining salon to tell them the ship was going in for a refit. The men from outside Liverpool would be paid off while the locals would be kept on the books.

The Chief Officer had been at sea for thirty-six years, having gone from school to become a cadet in the merchant marine, first on a four-masted cargo barque, and then on liners that took him to the Americas and the Mediterranean. In the First World War, he spent a year in the doomed campaign in the Dardanelles. Later, he would captain Cunard's most famous liners, the *Queen Elizabeth* and the *Queen Mary*, mingling with celebrities and statesmen on cruises and transatlantic voyages.

The son of a brewer from the market town of Stafford, Grattidge was a companionable man who disliked having to apply the more rigorous aspects of the Cunard disciplinary code – on one occasion, he excused a male and a female crew member who had broken regulations by being in a cabin together. Having dispatched the crew and completed other formalities, the solidly built, full-faced Chief Officer flipped a coin to decide whether to eat at a steak house or the best hotel in town, the massive, white painted Adelphi, with its colonnaded upper storeys and huge, chandeliered lounge. The coin having told him to go for the second, he headed up Hanover Street from the docks to enjoy a leisurely lunch in the ornately decorated dining room.

After his meal, Grattidge strolled back towards the docks in the afternoon sunshine. To while away the evening, he could choose between two top-line variety shows – one starring the 'wizard of the piano', Charlie Kunz, at the Empire, the other with the comic singing sisters, Elsie and Doris Waters, at the

Shakespeare. Then he planned to take a three-week break in the Lake District to get over the pressure and danger of the previous months.

As Grattidge passed the office of the Cunard Line behind the Port of Liverpool building at Pier Head, the Cunard Maritime Superintendent, a small, lively Welshman, hurried up to him.

'Thank God you're here,' he said. 'Big trouble. Get down to the ship and recall everyone. You haven't much time – you're sailing at midnight.'

Grattidge asked what the destination would be.

'The mission is urgent but unspecified,' was the only reply he got.

At that moment, the Chief Officer had a sense that something appalling was about to happen. Still, 'there was nothing I could do but obey orders'.

Some of the crew were still on board, including the Chief Engineer. Grattidge told him to get up steam. He telephoned Captain Sharp, and had telegrams sent to crew members who had left. 'You are urgently requested to return to ship immediately,' the cable read. 'Acknowledge. Master.'

Loudspeaker messages were broadcast at Liverpool railway stations telling those waiting for trains to go back to the ship. Others were contacted by telephone. All but three returned in time for the midnight departure. Among them was a Liverpool flyweight boxer, Joe Curran, who had joined the Merchant Navy. The youngest was a 14-year-old deck boy; the oldest a 74-year-old deck hand.

One of the *Lancastria*'s waiters was in a Liverpool pub with his mother and father when two plain-clothes detectives came in and asked if Joe O'Brien was there. After O'Brien identified himself, he was told to report back to the liner.

Walking down to the docks with his father, they met the ship's chef, Joe Pearse. O'Brien's father asked Pearse to look after his son. 'I sure will,' the chef replied.

A Canadian sailor, Michael Sheehan, was drinking at a pub in Canning Place in Liverpool when he heard that the *Lancastria* needed to gather together crewmen in a hurry. He headed for the docks, and signed on.

While the ship was in Glasgow, one of the liner's stewards, Tom Manning, had written to his brother-in-law, John, in Liverpool saying that he had got a job for him on board. Accompanied by his wife, John went to the docks on the night of 14 June intending to board the *Lancastria*. By the time they got to the quay, the ship was moving out. The couple stood and watched until she was out of sight.

Thomas Frodsham, known as 'Shorty', had been told by the *Lancastria*'s doctor to take time off for medical treatment. But no sooner had he reached his home in Birkenhead than he was informed that the liner was sailing that night. He asked his wife to pack him a small suitcase, and set off on the ferry back across the Mersey with his daughter, Leonora. Taking his leave, he assured her that he would be on deck beside a lifeboat at the first sign of trouble. 'Don't worry, and take care of your mum,' he told 18-year-old Leonora. Then she kissed him, and cried all the way home. They would never see one another again.

Built in Dalmuir in Scotland by the William Beardmore Company, the *Lancastria* made her maiden voyage for the Cunard Steamship Company to Canada in 1924. Originally called the *Tyrrhenia*, she was known to her sailors as the Soup Tureen. Her name was then altered to the less obscure

Lancastria. Though it might be easier to pronounce, the change was not welcome to the crew given the maritime superstition that doing this boded eventual disaster. But the worst that had happened to her was running aground on a pier in Liverpool harbour during a gale in 1936.

With a single funnel and two masts, the *Lancastria* was 582.5 feet long and seventy feet wide. She had five decks, the top one forty-three feet above the water line – the bridge from which Captain Sharp and Chief Officer Grattidge ran the vessel was another fifteen feet up. Her single funnel left room for 3000 square feet of deck for sports, bathing and sun. Her oil-burning engines meant that the top decks were free from the dust or cinders encountered on coal-fired ships. Advertisements made much of the way that white clothes could be worn for games of quoits and egg- and spoon-races without their wearers having to worry about being smudged by coal specks in the air.

There were two open-air swimming pools and a library stocked with the latest books. Special ventilators drew air down into staterooms. Her gymnasium had exercise bicycles, electrically powered horse-riding machines set to trot, canter or gallop, and a similarly designed electric camel whose use was said to be good for the figure.

The sixteen-foot-high dining room was decorated in Italian Renaissance style with semicircular arches set on small columns, a central dome, projecting balconies with wrought-iron fronts, and a thick carpet in geometric pattern. The ivory-white walls were inlaid with grey panels; the curtains were blue and gold. The verandah café resembled a courtyard garden, with trellis work, plants and wicker armchairs. The main lounge in French Renaissance style had oak panelling, mouldings, a barrel-vaulted ceiling, and a specially designed dance floor. The promenade deck was fitted with potted trees and wicker chairs. The smoking room was flanked with marble pillars, and lit by a chandelier.

The *Lancastria* was, one crewman recalled, a 'very, very happy ship'. But, despite her impressive interior, she was, by the standards of the top Blue Riband luxury liners that crossed the Atlantic in the 1930s, a bit small and a bit old. So she came to be used for cruises from New York to the Bahamas and the West Indies aimed at young American company managers, secretaries giving themselves a treat and honeymooning couples.

Receiving the call from Grattidge, Captain Sharp headed back across the Mersey from Birkenhead. He had taken command of the *Lancastria* only three months earlier. A solemn-looking and somewhat stout man of 5 feet 11 inches, Rudolph Sharp came from a seafaring family: his grandfather and uncle had both served with the Cunard Line, and one of his sons was in the navy. Graduating into the merchant marine in Liverpool in 1908, he had worked his way up on famous liners, including the *Lusitania*, which he captained until shortly before she was torpedoed in the Atlantic in 1915. He then commanded two other big liners, the *Mauretania* and *Olympia*, served on a third, the *Franconia*, and was staff captain on the *Queen Mary*. A Commander of the British Empire and member of the Royal Navy Reserve, Sharp sometimes appeared weary. He looked older than his fifty-five years.

With her captain and nearly all the crew on board, the order was given to sail down the west coast and round Cornwall to Plymouth. Nobody had any idea of their eventual destination, or why they had been called back to service.

Normally, the *Lancastria* blew her siren as she left Liverpool, but on 14 June 1940, she left silently, her departure cloaked in darkness.

Five weeks had passed since Adolf Hitler ended eight months of phoney war on his Western Front by launching what he called 'the most decisive battle for the future of the German nation'. Tanks, planes, artillery and infantry carved through the Netherlands and Belgium, outflanking the French by striking through the wooded hills of the Ardennes to avoid the supposedly impregnable fortifications of the Maginot Line. Sweeping north, the Wehrmacht drove back the British Expeditionary Force from its positions in Belgium and northeast France. Then, for reasons that have never been fully explained, Hitler had hesitated.

The commander at the front, General von Rundstedt, had recommended that the tank advance should be stopped so that the slower-moving infantry could catch up. His superiors, including the Commander-in-Chief, von Brauchitsch, told him to press on. But the Führer backed von Rundstedt. So the Panzers halted, and 330,000 British and Allied troops escaped from Dunkirk in what Winston Churchill, who had become Prime Minister in the middle of May, called 'a miracle of deliverance' and the *Daily Mirror* described in a headline as 'Bloody Marvellous'. Later, Hitler would say that he had wanted to spare Britain and to show that he was ready to reach a peaceful settlement. In fact, he may have believed that intense bombing raids by the Luftwaffe would force Britain to surrender – and have relished a chance to show his mastery over the army high command.

Behind them, the troops rescued in the armada of small

boats from Dunkirk left a country in collapse. The roads of France were clogged with refugees, moving through the summer heat in any form of transport available or, failing that, on foot. Millions fled the German advance. A Luftwaffe airman flying overhead described the scene below as 'desolate and dreadful'. The French pilot and writer, Antoine de Saint-Exupéry, compared it to a great anthill kicked over by a boot.

Refugees from the Low Countries poured into Paris by train, bewildered and seeking shelter in France.[2] At the Gare d'Austerlitz in the capital, 20,000 people were waiting for trains heading south at any one time. The crowd at the Gare Montparnasse, which served Brittany, stretched for a kilometre. The population of Lille, in the path of the German advance, dropped from 200,000 to 20,000. In the cathedral city of Chartres, only 800 of the 23,000 inhabitants stayed. In the eastern city of Troyes, thirty people remained.

Cars and lorries abandoned when they ran out of fuel stood on the roadside beside dead horses. Dive-bombing by Stuka planes added to the panic. So did rumours of fifth columnists, and of German paratroopers landing behind the lines disguised as nuns. The Interior Ministry questioned 62,000 suspected enemy agents, but detained only 500. In the northern town of Abbeville, twenty-two foreigners were shot out of hand.

With police joining the fleeing throng, law and order broke down. In one town in the Loiret department south of Paris, a local official reported that refugees were 'killing the chickens, the rabbits, the cattle [and] carrying off drinks and goods and bedclothes'. Families became separated on the road. Farmers demanded payment for water from their wells. 'Poor devils,' a British general wrote. 'It was a horrible sight.'

Blame for the collapse of France was laid on politicians, Communists, Jews and Freemasons as a proud nation sought reasons for its implosion, and the military leaders tried to explain away their inability to cope with the mechanised and aerial warfare pioneered by Germany. Military failure fostered an already latent sense of inferiority among the French in the face of resurgent Germany. Politicians were regarded with cynicism or contempt, and defeatism spread.

After Dunkirk, a new candidate joined the scapegoats. Britain, which had sent some half-a-million men to the continent following the declaration of war in September 1939, came to be depicted as an untrustworthy ally which had got France into the war and was now abandoning her at the crucial moment. A senior official remarked that, with the evacuation, Britain had already donned mourning clothes for France. Fearing the effect on morale, the high command asked Churchill not to say how many men had been taken off the beaches at Dunkirk – the Prime Minister declined to comply.

Though 100,000 of their soldiers had been among those evacuated, the French could only see the withdrawal as fresh proof of the validity of their description of Britain as a perfidious nation. The Permanent Under Secretary at the British Foreign Office, Sir Alexander Cadogan, noted that, if Britain did send men and planes back across the Channel, it would not 'prevent the French reviling us'.[3] The American journalist Clare Booth recorded growing hatred of the French for the English. The pro-appeasement French minister Paul Baudouin noted bitterly that Britain had saved 80 per cent of its men while France lost half of its troops.[4]

For the British, having got so many men home safely was a triumph in defeat despite the loss of 68,000 troops killed or captured in Belgium and France. For the French, it was made all the worse by the ringing declarations from Britain's Prime Minister that his nation would go on fighting whatever happened across the Channel; at one point, the French embassy in London made it known that it did not regard this as 'exactly encouraging' for its country's own efforts.

The Germans did all they could to sow discord among their opponents. Leaflets dropped by their planes and broadcasts by Nazi radio stations in French made much of the phrase *'filer à l'anglaise'* (to take French leave). Britain, it was said, would fight to the last Frenchman.

In London, the British Cabinet did not speak openly of a French defeat. Instead, ministers referred only to 'a certain eventuality' which, they feared, could lead to Britain being attacked from two directions – across the Channel from France, Belgium and the Netherlands, and over the North Sea from Norway. Reports from the war front made British generals increasingly pessimistic about their ally, and increasingly unwilling to send reinforcements back to France. In his diary, Alexander Cadogan reflected a widespread view when he wrote that, rather than dispatching help, 'I'd really rather cut loose and concentrate on defence of these islands.'[5]

Churchill, who was also Minister of Defence, was torn between two conflicting objectives. He wanted to keep France fighting, but he knew the need to conserve men and supplies – and, above all, planes – to defend Britain if the battle across the Channel was lost. The way France was crumbling could only arouse his worst fears. On 10 June, he set out for the airport to fly to Paris for a meeting with the French Prime Minister, Paul Reynaud. But he was told that the government had left the French capital, fearing it was about to fall to the Germans. 'What the Hell?' the Prime Minister said, and changed his plan to head for the Loire Valley where Reynaud and his ministers had set up temporary quarters.

On arrival at an airfield outside Orléans, Churchill walked around leaning on a stick; according to one observer, he was beaming as if this was the only place he wanted to be. However, his military liaison officer, General Edward Spears, noted that the French colonel who drove them from the airfield 'might have been welcoming poor relations to a funeral reception'. At the red brick Château du Muguet at Briare, east of Orléans, where the talks took place, the French sat with set white faces along one side of the conference table, their eyes cast down. 'They looked for all the world like prisoners hauled up from some deep dungeon to hear an inevitable verdict,' wrote Spears.[6]

They had every reason for pessimism. German tanks, spearheaded by General Erwin Rommel's fast-moving Panzers, were smashing their way forward. A third of France's 105 divisions had been lost. French generals had no idea how to wage the modern form of warfare now confronting them. They had been expecting a conflict in which their army would fight from static positions; instead they were dealing with a mobile, elusive enemy who was not tracked by their faulty intelligence. When the French evolved new battle plans to contain the foe, they found that German tanks had already gone beyond the lines they drew. The bombing and strafing attacks of Stuka planes added a new dimension to the campaign, particularly since much of the French air force had been destroyed on the ground. In despair, some generals broke down in tears while others stared at their maps as if totally lost.

Facing Churchill and his party at Briare sat the French

Commander-in-Chief, General Maxime Weygand, whose taunt skin and precise features gave him the look of an Oriental mandarin. Weygand had been called back from Syria to take the post three weeks earlier as the German advance made a mockery of the defensive plans of his predecessor, General Maurice Gamelin. The 73-year-old Weygand knew he had inherited a desperate situation. France had reached 'the last quarter of an hour,' he declared in an order of the day after assuming command.

The front, he told the British, was in a state of dislocation. He did not have a single battalion left in reserve. Exhausted men were deserting in droves. 'I am helpless,' Weygand told Churchill. As he listened, Spears found that his mouth had grown so dry that he could not swallow.[7]

Sitting hunched over at the conference table, twisting his ring, Churchill said all he could offer France was a Canadian division with seventy-two guns, which would be followed by another division ten days later. If France could hold out until the following spring, twenty to twenty-five divisions could be dispatched. Such a long timescale took no account of the situation on the battlefield, as everybody present knew all too well.

France's newly-appointed Deputy Defence Minister, Brigadier General Charles de Gaulle, who had led a tank unit in an unavailing attempt to stop the northern German advance at a battle round Abbeville, chain-smoked, lighting one cigarette from another and preaching resistance. But a much more weighty voice chipped in on the other side. Looking extremely pale and staring down at his hands spread on the table, France's Deputy Prime Minister, Philippe Pétain, was ready to admit defeat. The 84-year-old hero of the First World War Battle of Verdun, which had cost 700,000 casualties, said France was being smashed to pieces, and Britain had no chance of halting Germany if the French army failed to do so.

Weygand, a short-tempered man who grew impatient at any sign of opposition, returned to the charge. Dunkirk had deepened his distrust of the British who, he noted, could not resist 'the appeal of the ports'. 'Apart from his distinguished qualities,' he remarked on one occasion, 'the Englishman is motivated by an almost instinctive selfishness.' Yet Britain could redeem itself by sending all its fighter planes to France immediately. 'Now is the decisive moment,' he added.

'No,' Churchill replied after a pause. The decisive moment would come when Hitler hurled the Luftwaffe against Britain. 'If we can keep command of the air over our own island – that is all I ask – we will win it all back for you,' he added.

However great his sympathy for France and his desire to buttress his ally's morale, the vital consideration for the British Prime Minister was to retain the ability to keep fighting whatever the outcome across the Channel. In his first telephone conversation with Reynaud after taking office, Churchill had assured him that, whatever the French did, the British would continue to fight to the last. 'We shall go on to the end,' he declared in one of his most celebrated speeches that summer. 'We shall fight in France, we shall fight on the seas and the oceans, we shall fight with growing confidence and growing strength in the air, we shall defend our island whatever the cost may be, we shall fight on the beaches, we shall fight on the landing grounds, we shall fight in the fields and in the streets, we shall fight in the hills; we shall never surrender.' If the Nazis invaded Britain, he told colleagues, either they would be driven back, or he would be carried out dead from his office.

At a meeting of the Defence Committee in London on 8 June, Churchill had concluded it 'would be fatal to yield to the French demands and jeopardise our own safety'.[8] So it was not surprising that, when the French asked him at Briare what Britain would do if they capitulated and Germany focused its might across the Channel, the Prime Minister replied, in French, that he would drown as many of the invaders as possible and then '*frapper sur la tête*' those who crawled ashore. After which the British and French delegations had a light dinner, and went to bed.

The next morning, two French officers eating breakfast in the dining room of the château were taken aback when the big double doors opened. Standing there in a long flowing red silk kimono, his hair on end, was Churchill, asking about his morning bath.

Washed and dressed, the Prime Minister resumed the conference. The news from the battlefront was even worse. Weygand reported that some French divisions had just three or four guns; four had none at all. With the Germans only thirty miles from Paris, Churchill suggested that the city might put up resistance in the same way as Madrid had during the Spanish Civil War. 'To make Paris a city of ruins will not affect the issue,' Pétain responded, and Weygand declared the capital an open and undefended city to avoid bombing.

His doubts about France's will to resist reinforced, Churchill decided to fly home. He and his party were using a small pink plane, known as the Flamingo. The escort of fighters which had accompanied it from Britain the previous day was out of fuel, and supplies had not arrived by the time the Prime Minister was ready to leave. So the Flamingo flew alone. As it crossed the Channel, the cloud around it cleared. Below Churchill's plane, two German fighters were attacking a fishing boat. Their fliers did not look up and spot the unarmed aircraft.

Reporting to the War Cabinet on his return, Churchill said the Germans 'seemed to have over matched and outwitted' the French whose army was now on its last line.[9] 'Effective resistance by France as a great land power was coming to an end,' the Secretary for War, Anthony Eden, who had been at Briare, added. At the Foreign Office, Sir Alexander Cadogan noted in his diary: 'French howling for assistance . . . but it's so much down the drain.'[10]

Still, for Churchill, everything possible had to be done to postpone the day when France capitulated, not only out of his genuine feeling for the nation across the narrow sea but also because the longer it took Germany to defeat its neighbour, the more time Britain would have to build up its forces against the coming storm. So, on 13 June, as the *Lancastria* was sailing home to Liverpool from its mission to Iceland, the Prime Minister flew back to the Loire Valley for another meeting with Paul Reynaud at the French government's new headquarters.

Arriving at the airfield of the city of Tours at lunchtime, the British found that there was no welcoming party.[11] Churchill's pilot recalled that he 'looked as though he was trying to chew a mouthful of nuts and bolts'. He approached a group of French airmen, and told them his name, adding that he was the Prime Minister of Britain. He would, he said, be grateful for *une voiture*. The airfield commander's small Citroën was produced, and the five-man British party crammed itself inside, Churchill complaining that he had had no lunch and was very hungry. On the way into the city, they passed crowds of refugees before reaching the préfecture where they found the tough-minded Interior Minister, Georges Mandel, talking on two telephones at once as he tried to rally local officials to resist. Nobody knew where Reynaud was.

A French officer helped the British party to find a restaurant where they took a private room and ate cold chicken and cheese, washed down by the local Vouvray white wine. Eventually, Reynaud was found, and the meeting began in the préfecture. The diminutive 62-year-old Premier, his hair in a neat centre parting, showed his strain and exhaustion. The defeatists in the French government and high command were pressing him remorselessly to sue for peace, abetted by his domineering, pro-German mistress. The Premier's eyes twitched, and his face jumped with a tic, as he asked Churchill to release France from its undertaking not to make a separate peace with Berlin.

The British leader replied that he must discuss this with his colleagues alone. So they went out into the ill-kept rectangular garden of the préfecture, edging round puddles under rain-sodden trees, the surroundings matching their spirits. Returning to the meeting room, Churchill said that, though he understood the difficulties the French faced, he could not agree to the request. On leaving, Churchill saw Charles de Gaulle standing at the doorway, 'solid and expressionless'. '*L'homme du destin*,' the Prime Minister said in a low voice as he passed. The future head of the Free French remained impassive – if only because he had probably not heard the words.

That evening, the French Cabinet gathered in a château being used as the official residence of the President of the Republic, Albert Lebrun, an infirm 69-year-old who always hoped for the best – another politician said he 'cried whenever a cloud covered the sun'. He had every reason for tears now.

A fierce argument erupted between the Interior Minister, Mandel, and the Commander-in-Chief, Weygand, who flounced out. The pro-peace party made much of a linguistic misunderstanding arising from a remark by Churchill in French during the talks in Tours. When Reynaud had asked the Prime Minister what his attitude would be if France surrendered, Churchill had replied '*Je comprends*', intending to mean that he understood his ally's difficulties. But his words contained a dangerous ambiguity since they could be taken as indicating acquiescence. So they were promptly spun by proponents of ending the fighting as evidence that Britain agreed with the proposal to seek an armistice.

Later that night, General Spears saw Reynaud looking 'ghastly, with a completely unnatural expression, still and white'. His mistress stalked the corridors of the château where they were staying, throwing open doors to track down her man and press him to agree to yield to Hitler.

On 14 June, before leaving the Loire Valley for the greater security of Bordeaux, the French Premier sought help from across the Atlantic by sending a message to Franklin Roosevelt telling him that, unless he gave a firm undertaking that the United States would enter the war in the very near future, 'the destiny of the world will change'. But the President was running for re-election, and American public opinion was set against involvement in a European war – in one speech in the autumn, Roosevelt assured voters that 'your boys are not going to be sent into any foreign war'. It would be another eighteen months before Washington entered the conflict, and then only after being attacked at Pearl Harbor.

On the afternoon of 14 June, as the *Lancastria*'s crew was being summoned back to duty, the Germans entered Paris. The writer, André Maurois, said France had become a body without a head. Only 800,000 people remained in the city, a quarter of its peacetime population. The occupation troops behaved well, paying for food and offering their seats to old ladies on the Métro. But, with the soldiers came the first Gestapo agents, and Hitler made his aims quite clear: a new phase of the war was starting – 'the pursuit and final destruction of the enemy'. Unknown to the invaders, and unrecognised by their own government across the Channel, 150,000 of those enemy troops were lying in the path of the advancing Wehrmacht.

On 3 June, at the end of the exodus from Dunkirk, Churchill had told the War Cabinet that the troops of the British Expeditionary Force in France and Belgium 'had now been withdrawn to this country practically intact, except for their losses through casualties in combat'.[12] The following day, a report to the War Cabinet said it was 'possible that a certain number of men might be trying to make their way back independently in a south-westerly direction'. The First Sea Lord chipped in to say that the navy was keeping a watch for individual British soldiers who might reach the French coast.

A confidential annexe to the Cabinet minutes did note that the Secretary of State for War was anxious to withdraw remaining divisions south of the Somme which had been out of the main line of the German advance. But, as far as everybody in Britain was concerned, the BEF had come home on the armada of small ships. That impression remains in place six decades later – one recent history of the fall of France written by an eminent British historian records that 'after Dunkirk, there was hardly any further British army presence on the Continent' except for a Highland division which was still in France after retreating from the Saarland.[13]

Churchill's government had every reason to encourage the belief that Dunkirk had drawn a line under the disastrous opening of the war. With France about to be defeated, the evacuation marked the end of the beginning, a manifestation of unquenchable spirit by a nation standing united against the technological prowess of the Luftwaffe and the Wehrmacht.

The reality was very different. The British troops who 'might' be trying to get away from the Germans were far from being the scattered individuals suggested by the War Cabinet reports.

In all, 150,000 British troops were left across the Channel – almost half as many as had been taken off from Dunkirk. There were also 85,000 Poles fighting on French soil.

Some of the British soldiers still in France had failed to get to Dunkirk, or had not been told of the evacuation; some had been cut off from the Channel by the German push northwards from the Ardennes. But most had not been near the battles of May and early June. Many were support troops, in what were known as Lines of Communication units, engineers, repair men, transport and communications staff, wireless operators, RAF ground crews, NAAFI store minders, cooks, bakers, pay clerks and guards for arms and supply depots.

They were often poorly armed, and had received little or no combat training. The British high command showed scant interest in them – they were referred to as 'the Grocers'.

Many had been stationed in areas which had not been attacked, or had moved away from the main line of the enemy advance. One unit of the Royal East Kent Regiment spent a month being shuttled round France by rail in cattle trucks without seeing any fighting – its men were led to understand that a second British Expeditionary Force was on its way and that they would join it. The senior officers of one RAF unit, whose airfield was guarded by French soldiers armed with rifles dating from the war of 1870 against Germany, drove about in a Bentley, at one point saving the life of the gunner from a downed German plane whom French peasants had wanted to kill with their farm implements.

Three divisions saw action at the collapsing front. One of them, the 51st Highland Division made an excellent impression on the British commander, General Henry Karslake. But he was shocked by others he came across. 'Their behaviour was terrible!' he noted.[14] 'From all sides I heard that this was typical of the New Army Discipline, as a result of the Democratising of the Army.' General Karslake also came to the conclusion that the men were being given excessive quantities of rations.

After withdrawing from their original position in the Saar, the Highlanders had been isolated from the rest of the BEF by the German drive for the coast. They were dog tired, and their numbers were depleted by battle casualties. The commander, General Victor Fortune, called the front he was meant to hold south of the Channel coast 'ridiculous'. His 'dead beat' men, he noted in a letter, had not had a proper night's rest for six weeks.[15] The remnants of one battalion had sheltered under hedges from an air attack for ten minutes – as the bombs fell, the commanding officer and half his men fell asleep.

'I feel it is time we explained to the [French] Commander-in-Chief and Army Commander that there is a limit to gambling with troops on a wide frontage,' Fortune added in a report. 'Also please some air [support]! . . . Forgive me for being vindictive but I do not want to see 51st destroyed and useless for the future which it will be at the present rate. I am quite willing to ask them for a good deal, but I think they have been asked for too much.' Weygand took to calling the Highlanders' commander 'Misfortune'.[16]

The division was ordered to head for the Channel coast to be evacuated. Its original destination was Le Havre, but this was switched to the small Norman port of St-Valéry-en-Caux. A fleet of rescue ships set out to pick it up. Most of the boats lacked wireless communications and, when fog covered the sea, they were cut off from one another. Forty thousand French troops on the flank surrendered, and Rommel's Panzers occupied St-Valéry before the Highlanders could embark, shutting them into an isolated pocket. A few British troops escaped by running for six miles under machine-gun and mortar fire until they reached the port of Veules-les-Roses where ships were waiting. In all, this evacuation fleet took off 2137 British and 1184 French troops. But General Fortune was forced to surrender, and was photographed looking disconsolate on the quayside with a smiling Rommel beside him. Eight thousand British soldiers were taken prisoner. Churchill called it a 'brutal disaster'. Half a century later, a granite monument was erected on the towering white cliffs overlooking the pebble beach from which the Scottish division had not escaped, with the inscription 'In proud and grateful memory of the 51st (Highland) Division who gave their lives during the war 1939–45'. Down below, one of the main streets in St-Valéry is named *l'Avenue de la 51ème.*

An ill-equipped scratch force known as the Beauman Division, from the name of its commander, was put together from various British units to help defend the Norman capital of Rouen on the River Seine. Thinly stretched over a fifty-mile front, it was told to destroy bridges, and lay anti-tank mines. A sergeant with the division noted in his diary that, as they moved to the front, they passed a stream of French refugees who put their thumbs up, 'even the kids'. In villages, girls blew them kisses. But they were soon swept back by the Panzer advance – in all, the division had just twenty anti-tank guns.

Further forward, the 1st Armoured Division, which had been sent to France in the spring, had never had time to organise itself properly. One brigade only got its equipment a day or two before crossing the Channel. Bicycles for messengers were still in their wrappings. None of the men had been trained to fire an anti-tank gun.[17]

The divisional commander, Roger Evans, decided to make a stand on the railway east of Rouen. Weygand told him that the struggle for the city would be decisive. Since the French could not produce any more troops for their Tenth Army in the sector, the outcome would depend on the 1st Armoured, he added.

Evans pointed out the extreme weakness of his force which faced far heavier and more numerous German tanks. Weygand replied that, if the British could not stop the enemy with its armoured vehicles, they 'must stop him with bare hands and bite him like a dog'.

As the Tenth Army disintegrated, Evans prepared to retreat across the Seine. He watched French soldiers pouring to the rear, and looked in vain for any spirit of resistance. 'No defences were prepared,' a British report read. 'No wire or anti-tank mines were sited and no trenches were dug. Nor was there apparently any offensive spirit among commanders or troops . . . it is not too much to say that an atmosphere of inevitable defeat was growing.'

In adversity, relations between senior officers in the Allied armies grew frayed. A French general accused Beauman of cowardice, and dismissed his soldiers as 'a thoroughly undisciplined rabble'. Another said Victor Fortune was guilty of treachery, and should be court-martialled. Karslake concluded that this was part of 'a definite policy instigated by General Weygand', presumably to find a scapegoat for the reverses suffered by his own forces.

In a bid to raise French morale, a Canadian division left Britain to cross the Channel. Landing at Brest, it moved through the Breton capital of Rennes and headed for the city of Laval on the line of the German advance. But, at the same time, Operation Cycle was launched to move more than 12,000 troops by sea from the big port of Le Havre in Normandy to the greater safety of Cherbourg on the peninsula sticking out into the Channel. Sixty-seven merchant ships and 140 small craft were drafted in for the task. The nature and pace of the German campaign made military planning difficult, and Churchill said the British forces should no longer accept orders from the French 'who had let us down badly'. But, while the front-line soldiers were either evacuated or captured, more than 100,000 of their comrades were still forgotten in France.

Some of them followed the progress of the war by listening to the radio or picking up copies of the *Continental Daily Mail* they found in shops in towns near their bases before the occupation of Paris. Alec Cuthbert, a carpenter from Holbeach in Lincolnshire serving with a vehicle repair unit outside Nantes, heard of the German advance on the BBC, but still 'hadn't a clue about what was going on'.

Many remained in the dark about the progress of the fighting or depended on the rumour mill. Some had not even heard about the evacuation from Dunkirk. 'My time in France was nothing but retreat, anxiety, lack of knowledge of what was going on, communications were almost non-existent, fighter control as such had vanished,' an RAF fighter pilot recalled.

Writing in a black-covered copy of the *Stockfeeder's Diary*, wireless operator Mervyn Llewelyn-Jones noted:

> June 9. War news grave. Germans in Sessions [Soissons]. Sent 10/- note home on 5th of June to Darling Nan.
>
> June 10. Bought Daily Mail. Up at 7am. Extremely hot today. Germans nearing Rouen. Italy coming in on German side.
>
> June 12. Went for a bath. Changed socks. Stayed in Barracks. Went over to Canteen. No letters today. Rather a dull day.
>
> June 13. Return of washing. Changed clothes. Wrote to my Darling also Dad and Mam.
>
> June 14. Two loving letters from my Darling – all is well. Little Michael doing well. Good news. Paid 50 fr.[18]

Neville Chesterton, a 19-year-old former railway clerk from Wednesbury in Staffordshire, who found France very flat and uninteresting, sensed that nobody knew where his fifty-strong Royal Engineers unit was going or what it was meant to be doing. As the men headed westwards towards the Atlantic coast, they heard rumours that the fighting was going badly, though the word 'Dunkirk' was not mentioned. Eventually they reached a camp thirty miles from the port of St-Nazaire where they practised rifle shooting and undertook guard duties. German planes flew very high overhead from time to time, but they saw no RAF aircraft. 'This is a most peculiar war,' Lance Corporal Chesterton thought, 'nothing seems to be happening.'

On the other side of the country, a few RAF units were still operating in eastern France, and men gathered at one airfield to see off the New Zealander ace, 'Cobber' Kain, a glamorous figure who had chalked up seventeen 'kills' of enemy planes and was engaged to a well-known actress. He was heading back to England for leave. Before departing, he gave a flying display in his Hurricane. As he made a low roll, the tip of one wing hit the ground, the plane crashed and Kain was killed – not having heard the news, men on the hull of the *Lancastria* would call desperately for him to fly in to shoot down the German planes strafing them.

Some of those fleeing the enemy were caught in streams of refugees that were attacked by German dive bombers, their sirens sending out terrifying banshee screams as they swooped. A British dispatch rider found himself in a traffic jam at a village crossroads when the planes attacked. Swept from his motorcycle by the impact of the explosions, he landed beside a boy of about five whose legs had been blown off and who had been blinded in one eye. Taking the child in his arms, the soldier could see that he was dying in terrible pain; so he drew his revolver and shot him – the memory drove him mad.

Many of the British troops moving from the east of France to greater safety in the west were in organised convoys of vehicles, or were put on trains. But some went freelance. A sergeant from an RAOC Light Aid Detachment stole a bicycle and rode across France from Lille; on the way, he saw a group of men from the Pioneer Corps attacking German tanks with their picks and shovels.

At the wheel of his wireless truck, 21-year-old Leonard Forde became separated from his convoy as it headed out of eastern France. Strafing attacks forced him to jump repeatedly from the cab on his lorry, known in service slang as a 'gin palace'. With his crew, he took to small roads to escape enemy attention. Life became a game of hide-and-seek. Reaching Le Mans, he began to operate the truck's wireless monitoring gear. As his radio chattered away in high speed Morse code, he noticed that the strong signals all had German call signs. It was time to move further west.

Wilfred Oldham's Royal Signals unit had been sent to the Champagne town of Bouzy-sur-Marne to work with RAF detachments posted to eastern France before the German advance. He and his colleagues were housed in the premises of the Moët et Chandon wine firm: Wilf's office was above the grape presses. Across the road was the headquarters of another great champagne house, Veuve Clicquot. The British bought champagne for nine pence a bottle.

At the end of May, the unit was ordered to withdraw. Under the command of an Australian major, the men took a dozen new American-made lorries from an abandoned air force base, filling the tanks with petrol and arming themselves with a dozen Lewis guns. Having no idea of where to head, they wandered round northern France. On the way, they ran into some French troops who told them about Dunkirk. After reaching Le Mans, their commander suggested driving to St-Nazaire. Their improvised journey to the west was typical of the independent British units seeking a way out of France, ultimately taking them to the last escape hatch left.

William Philip Knight, who would be so frightened by the sight of a man disappearing in flames below the oily sea off St-Nazaire, was a sergeant in a General Construction Company of the Royal Engineers and an explosives expert. At the Dunkirk evacuation, his six-man group was detailed to patrol the perimeter of a British position in a lorry loaded with explosives to use against the advancing enemy. On 1 June, they staged an ambush for German tanks and motorcyclists. But their rifles were no match for the tanks, and they were forced to retreat, abandoning their lorry when it broke down.

Missing the evacuation from the beaches, they found themselves in a village which came under German attack. The six men dived into a cellar of a demolished house. They discussed whether to surrender, but decided to stay where they were. Early the next morning, Knight climbed the stairs from the cellar to see what was happening outside. The sky was black with planes dropping bombs. Looking down to the harbour, he saw clouds of dust and smoke, flying bricks and debris. For the first time in his life, he felt afraid, realising that only an Act of God would save them.

Just then, Knight heard a scurry of feet. Two civilians covered in muck and dust practically fell on him at the top of the stairs. The three of them went down into the cellar. Then one of the Frenchmen, who spoke quite good English, guided them to safety through back lanes and small holdings; at one point, they crossed a canal by climbing over trucks which had been tipped into the water.

The next morning, the men got back to their lorry which they repaired. They drove off towards the inland town of Hesdin, turning off the road in the evening, intending to spend the night hidden in a wood. At that moment, they heard the noise of engines coming down the road – a procession of captured French and British trucks driven by Germans.

Counting on being taken for part of the convoy to get through the lines, the British joined up as the last vehicle. They drove for about forty miles without lights, and passed the enemy sentry posts. Nobody challenged them – the darkness hid their uniforms.

Having got to temporary safety, they peeled off from the convoy and went west, their lorry still carrying its load of explosives. Bypassing Abbeville where the battle was raging, they got over the River Somme. Then they headed cross-country to Normandy, using small country roads to avoid the Germans. On one occasion, their progress blocked by the destruction of a bridge, they cut down trees to enable them to get across a small river. Along the way, they met soldiers from the 51st Highland Division en route for St-Valéry, but decided to go off on their own rather than heading there.

French and Belgian stragglers joined the party to swell it to about thirty. One day, coming round a corner, they saw tanks, and German troops grouped round the armoured vehicles. Getting as close as they could, they threw hand grenades and fired their guns at the enemy. One man clambered up on a tank, and dropped a grenade inside. Then William Knight and his comrades retreated with three Germans prisoners, whom they handed over to a group of French soldiers having lunch in a field on a table set with a cloth.

Moving further west, Knight's unit ran into more German armoured vehicles and motor cyclists with machine guns who took them captive. They were ordered to sit on the side of the narrow road while the armoured cars drove off, leaving two motorcyclists to watch the prisoners.

Knight shouted out insults about Germans in English to test whether the guards spoke his language. There was no response, so he told the others that he was going to jump a guard, and that they should deal with the second man. Taking out his cigarette case, he tried to lure the first guard close to him by offering him a cigarette; but the German did not smoke. Then Knight indicated that he wanted to defecate. The guard signalled his agreement. Going to a bush, Knight started to undo his trousers. The guard came across to watch him. Knight leaped at the man, and got his arm round his throat. The rest of the unit jumped on the other guard, battering him to death.

As Knight put his weight on top of the first man's gun, the German drew a trench knife from his boot. The blade went through the Englishman's hand, and into his chin. Fighting for his life, Knight found the guard's jugular, and pressed it till he passed out.

The party got into its truck, drove to the main road and turned left towards Rouen. His companions wrapped field dressings round Knight's bleeding wounds. On the way, the truck sped past advancing Germans, and got across a bridge over the Seine to join British troops south of the river.

Not wanting to be caught there, they headed off again, aiming for the ancient town of Beauvais. Hearing that the Germans had taken it, they went south towards Compiègne. However, that, too, was about to fall, so they drove to the walled city of Senlis where they handed some of their explosives to the French army to help blow up a house that would impede the defenders' field of fire. In return, they were given a lot of nasty wine.

They debated trying to get to Switzerland, but decided to drive the fifty miles to Paris, instead. On 11 June, on the way to the capital, Knight passed his thirtieth birthday. That night, they were put up in a farmhouse where they enjoyed a bath and a good hot dinner. Two days later, they got to the suburbs of Paris – just as the Germans were entering the city from the other side. So they decided to go west, reaching Le Mans on 14 June, and staying the night at a big British army dump that had been set up on the motor race track, the first part of their escape from Dunkirk completed.

For some British units, the retreat was eased with the local wines or stronger alcohol. Military canteens and NAAFI stores had been left open, and men were taking what they could find. The driver of one air force lorry got so drunk that he could not stand up even after his head was held under a cold water tap. More soberly, others crammed sweets and cigarettes from Salvation Army shops into their kitbags. A Royal Engineers unit found a radio in one abandoned store, and got its first news of Dunkirk by listening to Churchill's speech announcing that the BEF had been successfully evacuated from France.

Outside Orléans, Sergeant Macpherson, who would share his life jacket with a man who could not swim as they escaped from the sinking *Lancastria*, was posted to an RAF base on a tributary to the River Loire at the village of Olivet. He and his colleagues regularly crossed the Loiret in a dinghy to what he recalled as 'a road house with a funny English name' to eat and drink white wine. Returning one night, Macpherson took up the stance of a Viking figurehead at the front of the little boat, brandishing two litre wine bottles; when his companions rocked the dinghy, he fell into the water.

As the Germans advanced towards Orléans, most of the RAF men headed west. Left behind to burn the unit's papers, Macpherson crossed the Loiret for the last time on his own in the dinghy to eat two pâté de foie gras sandwiches at the roadhouse, washed down by white wine. He finished off with liqueurs, each glass costing him the equivalent of three pence.

While eating his sandwiches, he got into conversation with an American woman who had worked in a British servicemen's club in Paris. She told him how bad the military situation was. Leaving her, Macpherson rowed back across the river to burn more documents. Then he borrowed a bicycle to go to a nearby village to collect food and drink. The road was crowded with refugees; at one point, a car knocked him off his bicycle.

Macpherson drank more wine in the village, and then rode back to join the remaining members of his unit whom he found at the base eating enormous doorstep sandwiches of corned beef, and sharing huge mugs of strong, scalding tea. Feeling rather ill, he got into the back of a big French army lorry where he found a large armchair, in which he sat down to rest.

Further west, life was uneventful for British troops stationed in and around Nantes, a major port sitting astride the wide River Loire, forty miles from the sea with elegant avenues and squares of eighteenth-century houses built on the proceeds of the slave trade. Jack Ratcliffe, of the Royal Ordnance Corps, who worked as a clerk in a warehouse, recalled that the daily routine consisted of 'drill, breakfast, drill, parade to depot, lunch, parade back, until 5.30 p.m., march back for mug of tea, bread and cheese, fill in sandbags to defend the city, working until dark'. On Sunday, they went to the Protestant church. Generally, they were 'having fun, all men together'.

Major Fred Hahn passed his time watching tennis at the city's university stadium. A First World War veteran from Cheadle in Lancashire and commander of a divisional ordnance workshop, Hahn made contact with the local fraternity of Masons, and joined them in a group photograph, the Mayor sitting in the middle of the front row.

Though the Nazi propagandist William Joyce, Lord Haw-Haw, had warned that the British camps in Nantes would be bombed, there was no sign of the enemy. French newspapers and the radio reproduced optimistic military communiqués or simply told readers, '*Rien à signaler*' – 'Nothing to report.' Everybody believed that the great Maginot defensive line along the traditional German invasion route would hold the enemy back with its huge concrete emplacements, heavy guns and underground railways. In Nantes, the British met at their club as usual, and life was calm.

Then the refugees started to arrive on trains and down the roads along the Loire. The first, from Belgium, were no particular cause for concern – everybody knew fighting was going on there. But, before long, people began to come from northern France, and, one resident recalled, 'horror of horrors from Paris'. Fifth columnists stirred up anxiety, and German planes flew over the city.

Donald Draycott, the RAF ground crewman from Derbyshire who was to be surprised at how calm he felt as he watched people jumping off the sinking *Lancastria*, sensed some hostility from the local people when he visited the main theatre in Nantes. Also, 'when a bus came along and the bus was pretty well full, they'd push you out of the queue and get on themselves,' he recalled. But then, he reflected: 'I think it's part of the French characteristics, they did it to others as well.'

Horace Lumsden, who had left school at fifteen-and-a-half to join the Ordnance Corps as a bugler and clerk, had been in Nantes since the first BEF base was established in the city in 1939. He had celebrated his twenty-third birthday there at the beginning of June. He found the French very friendly, particularly the wife of the owner of the Café des Jardinières, but he noted some friction, too. In part, this was because the British troops were better paid than their French counterparts, and so had more money to spend.

There was also rivalry over female company. Many local men had gone to the front, leaving their wives alone. Some foreign soldiers had affairs with Frenchwomen – one resulted in the birth of a son months after the British had left. French families sometimes objected to these liaisons on behalf of the absent husbands or boyfriends. One of Horace Lumsden's fellow soldiers was at a young woman's house when a relative came round with friends. She was married, and her husband was away with his unit. The Frenchman beat the British trooper so badly that his face was reduced to a mass of pulp.

Nantes and St-Nazaire had been used to bring supplies and vehicles into France since the outbreak of war, and the British set up a network of support and repair bases in the area. In the Gâvre Forest, they laid down a roadway of stones and concrete foundations for hangars and for two block houses. By a dirt track in another forest, a unit from the Royal Engineers went to work to build a railway line. Next to their headquarters was a small farmhouse. The farmer's wife cooked the soldiers eggs and chips. Her 13-year-old son, Laurent Couedel, whom the troops called Laurie, watched the men at work, striking up a friendship as he chatted in French they could not understand.

One base was in St-Etienne de Montluc, a large village with a small château and an imposing white calvary beside the railway line to St-Nazaire and the Atlantic coast. The men of the Number One Heavy Repair Shop of the Royal Army Service Corps repaired damaged vehicles brought in by rail, and serviced vehicles from Britain, in workshops set up in the pigsties of an abandoned farm.

The 400 men were a cheerful group, taking as their emblem Happy from the Seven Dwarfs, whom they depicted carrying a spanner and a brace inside a circle inscribed with the motto 'Whistle While You Work'. They drank and ate fish and chips in the Lion d'Or café opposite the large stone church. A touring concert party entertained them for a time. French women cooked their rations into tasty meals in local homes. At Christmas, they marched through the streets, and attended a midnight mass that seemed to go on for ever – afterwards, there was an early breakfast in the village. The soldiers spoke no French when they arrived, but learned a few words including 'Voulez-vous promener avec moi?' to say to the local girls.

The barn where the repair men slept with a view of the sky through holes was baptised 'Holden's Hotel', apparently after one of their number – a sign with the name was put up outside the door. To wash off the grease and dirt after the day's work, they heated water in a big pot on a stove – but it did not go far. Their latrines were in the field alongside. In the lavatory one day, one of the mechanics, Stan Flowers, found a copy of the *Faversham News*, from his home town in Kent. He made inquiries, and discovered that there was another Faversham man in the unit, called Walter James

Smith, whose mother ran a hairdresser's in the main street of the town. They met up, and became fast friends.

A communal mess hall was set up for all the troops posted to St-Etienne. Outside was a sty for a pig which the local people had given to the British troops. Each morning, the soldiers fed it porridge after calling out 'Morning, Pig.' One day, the pig looked grumpy.

'What's wrong, Pig?' one man called out.

'Not enough sugar in the porridge,' another replied.

Despite their tranquil lives, some of the men grew concerned at the way the war was going. Alec Cuthbert, the carpenter from Lincolnshire who heard about the German advance on the BBC, could not understand why they were not being evacuated. There was no way the unit could resist the Panzers if they reached St-Etienne. But, instead of being moved, they were called out on parade each morning as though everything was normal.

The Pay Corps private Sidney Dunmall, who would be pulled free from the suction of the sinking *Lancastria* on a plank, was posted to the small town of Pornichet on the coast just west of St-Nazaire. He had read about Dunkirk in the *Continental Daily Mail,* and had been to the cinema to see a Deanna Durbin film, *Three Smart Girls.* He and his friends ate in a forces canteen run by a local woman in a château at the end of a long drive. They found the eggs and chips served there very nice. One day, the woman shrieked: 'Paris has fallen. Paris has fallen. What are we going to do? All is lost.'

Dunmall and his friends went to the counter to console her. They said they had heard that a large contingent of

Canadians was arriving at Cherbourg. 'Don't worry,' they told her. 'It's not the end.' What they did not know was that the Canadians had been turned round and sent back to Britain in the face of the German advance.

As the men walked up the drive after finishing their meal, their duty sergeant rode in on his bicycle, shouting: ' Where the Hell have you been? Get back to your billets immediately. There's a flap on.'

They hurried to their billets in the Hôtel des Étrangers, but no orders were awaiting them, so they went to bed – Dunmall shared a four-poster with four or five other men. During the night, an air-raid warning sounded. They got up and their sergeant major commanded them to go out into the road without stopping to get dressed. So they formed up in the drizzling rain, some in their pyjamas. The sergeant major marched them a couple of hundred yards to slit trenches half full of water. Sheltering there, they heard a throbbing noise overhead, followed by a tremendous explosion. When everything was quiet, they went back to bed. In the morning, they saw a big crater in the beach.

Trainloads of wounded British soldiers had begun to arrive in the area, awaiting evacuation. In the smart resort of La Baule, up the coast, the top hotel, the half-timbered Hermitage, was converted into a hospital. The owner of the local casino, M. André, provided another building where medical services were organised by Joan Rodes, a 23-year-old Englishwoman from Portsmouth married to a French army officer who was away at the front. Rodes knew La Baule well from holidays spent with her family-in-law at their villa there. Initially, she and her three staff cared for French refugees, but, before long, hundreds of wounded British were in the town.

In the shipbuilding port of St-Nazaire, the British set up a regional garrison command in a villa in the tree-lined Rue Marcel Sembat. Headed by Colonel V. T. R. Ford, DSO, it had twelve staff, including a lieutenant colonel, six majors, and three captains. There was also an army chaplain. Its area of responsibility ran along the Atlantic coast from the fishing port of Pornic to the south, through St-Nazaire to La Baule, and then up the River Vilaine to the town of La Roche-Bernard.

On 4 June, the garrison's diary recorded rumours that St-Nazaire was about to be bombed.[19] But no planes appeared.

On 5 June, the British officers turned their attention to finding a camp site for a corps of Indian Mules consisting of 300 men and 400 animals, which had been left behind in France. A French naval captain paid an official call to discuss defensive measures. Two platoons of British troops were posted to the airfield in case the enemy tried a parachute landing there. Fourteen light-machine-gun posts were placed on the docks. A second Church of England chaplain, the Reverend Holt, arrived.

On 6 June, a hospital ship, the *Dorsetshire*, took on a thousand wounded men, and sailed off in the evening.

For 7 and 8 June, as the *Lancastria* was returning from Norway and the French government was burning its papers before leaving Paris, the garrison diary recorded simply: 'Nothing of note.' The following day, three hospital trains arrived at La Baule. Most of the wounded were from the battle at Abbeville.

On 10 June, as Italy entered the war, Colonel Ford, the garrison commander, called on the Mayor of St-Nazaire to discuss defensive measures. During the next two days, as Churchill met the French in Briare, the Colonel inspected a submarine depot and the defences of the ancient town of Redon. At 10 p.m. on 12 June, a German plane dropped a single bomb near the St-Nazaire marshalling yard, damaging the track and several wagons. One, containing oil, caught fire. There were no casualties.

On 13 June, once again, there was 'Nothing of note.'

The next day, everything suddenly changed. Officers were called to a conference to consider the 'possibility' of an evacuation of the British Expeditionary Force. In Nantes, Major Fred Hahn reckoned that 'the balloon is about to go up' but, 'as a responsible officer', he made no entry to this effect in his diary. Up the River Loire in Olivet, Sergeant Macpherson was sitting in the armchair in the back of the lorry as his unit drove away through the night from its base, five hours before the Germans entered Orléans.

Further north, Joe Sweeney's regiment had been ordered to leave the base it had occupied outside Le Havre for the past four-and-a-half months. Sweeney, a 21-year-old, fair-haired Scot who had worked at the City Treasurer's office in Newcastle-upon-Tyne before being called up, drove a Humber Snipe staff car in a convoy of vehicles carrying supplies to safety. He crossed the Seine on a ferry, heading west. In the evening, a car carrying the unit's colonel passed him. Sweeney spoke fluent French, and the officer told him to go to a nearby farm to ask the farmer's wife to make a meal. The two men and the colonel's driver enjoyed an excellent dinner, well washed down with wine. In return, Sweeney presented the farmer's wife with a dozen tins of bully beef and tinned beans from his supplies.

In a move typical of the dislocation of the time, the convoy was suddenly told to turn round and go east back to the Seine: it took twenty-four hours to get formed up to take the new course. Sweeney used the delay to hitch a lift in a French van to the town of Evreux, where he had another good meal, and visited the main church to say a prayer. The first car to stop for him on the way back was that of his colonel, who had also gone into town for a meal. The two men sat on the back seat of the car, the young man feeling 'like a lord' as he chatted with his commanding officer.

The next morning, after sleeping in or under the vehicles, everybody had breakfast of bacon and eggs, served in billycans. By 8 a.m., they were driving east. Along the way, they passed a French military airfield which was being bombed by German Stukas. They dived into ditches and watched five French fighters take off, only to be shot down before reaching cruising altitude.

When the Stukas had gone, the British drove back to the Seine where they camped by a promontory overlooking Rouen. During the night, Sweeney counted forty-one German planes flying through ground fire to bomb bridges. The group spent five days by the river, collecting equipment from an abandoned British army depot which had been left in such a rush that there were unfinished meals in the mess tent. The equipment was put on a train, but was destroyed by a Luftwaffe raid.

An hour before midnight on 10 June, Sweeney and his comrades heard that the Germans had crossed the Seine, and were approaching their base. They boarded trains to go west again, stopping at Le Mans to pick up coal. There, Sweeney filled water bottles for himself and the five other men in his compartment from the big pipes used for the locomotive. The water was muddy and dirty, so he put in purification tablets, adding fruit salts to take away the nasty taste.

After a slow journey interrupted by frequent stops, the men eventually arrived in Nantes where they were taken to a big mess hall for a meal, the officers and chaplain sitting at the top table. As everybody stood for grace, the fruit salts went to work, and Sweeney dashed to the lavatory.

His unit was billeted in a camp on a football field in the city. There were no inspections or work to do. So the men passed the time as best they could. Visiting a museum, Sweeney spotted a German First World War helmet, and asked whether he could have it. The curator said yes, and the young man carried it off as a war trophy.

As the days passed, Sweeney got into the habit of going to the railway station buffet for morning coffee, and to watch the arrival of refugees. One day, five trains rolled in one after another. Among the passengers pouring on to the platform, Sweeney noticed a woman he had met in Le Havre.

She was Thérèse van Looche, the daughter of Belgians who had moved to France during the First World War. She had been in the typing pool at the harbour station in Le Havre, where she had become friendly with a British soldier called Les Stevenson, whom Sweeney knew. Les' job was to write out vouchers and take them to be typed up. As their friendship blossomed, he began to take all his vouchers to Thérèse.

Sweeney went out to meet her, and she asked: '*Mais où est Les?*' Sweeney led her to the main door of the station, and pointed out the Café de la Gare across the road. If she was waiting inside at 5 p.m. that afternoon, Les would arrive, he assured her.

Heading back to the British base, Sweeney went looking for his friend, telling everyone he met from his unit that, if they saw him, they should tell him to be at the café at 5 p.m. Getting the word, Les turned up at the appointed hour. Joe and five others were waiting outside.

Sweeney opened the door, saying to his friend: '*Après vous!*'

'Oh no Joe!' Les replied. 'After you!'

The half-dozen soldiers pushed Les inside. Then they closed the door, and went off to another café.

General Alan Brooke was less than pleased when he was sent back to France in the middle of June. The 57-year-old soldier, who would go on to become Britain's Chief of Staff, had helped to command the evacuation from Dunkirk, sleeping for thirty-six hours after he reached his home in Hampshire. Then he was called to the War Office to be told he was going across the Channel to organise British troops left there to resist the German advance.

Brooke, who had been brought up in south-west France by his mother who preferred that country to Britain, recorded that this was one of his blackest moments. 'I knew only too well the state of affairs that would prevail in France from now onwards,' he wrote in his diary. 'I had seen my hopes in the French Army gradually shattered ... I had witnessed the realisation of my worst fears concerning its fighting value and morale and now I had no false conceptions as to what its destiny must inevitably be. To be sent back again into that cauldron with a new force to participate in the final stages of French disintegration was indeed a dark prospect.'[20]

He asked the Chief of the Imperial General Staff, Sir John

Dill, if he could refit two of the divisions which had come back from Dunkirk and take them with him to provide experienced troops. There was no time, he was told. When the Secretary for War, Anthony Eden, enquired if he was satisfied with what was being done, Brooke replied that his mission had no military value, could not accomplish anything, and had every probability of turning into a disaster.

Leaving Southampton at night on 12 June, Brooke sailed to Cherbourg on a dirty Dutch steamer – there was no food on board, but Brooke's wife had made him sandwiches. In a further sign of the dislocation and the bad state of Allied relations, the French harbour authorities would not let him disembark for several hours. When he did get ashore in heavy rain, it was in the middle of an air raid. To make things worse, the local British command had not been told that the General was coming. It was, Brooke noted, 'a very unpleasant return trip'.[21]

At 8 a.m. the next day, he set off on a six-hour drive to British headquarters at Le Mans, his journey much slowed down by refugees on the road. On arrival, Brooke took over command of all British troops in France, telling his predecessor, Henry Karslake, to fly home immediately. Then he continued his journey south to meet the French Commander-in-Chief in the government's temporary resting place at Tours.

Maxime Weygand was away for the day, and, when they met the following morning, he said the French were no longer capable of organised fighting. Resources were exhausted. Many formations worn out. Organised defence had come to an end. The commander, who had injured his neck in a car crash, looked very wizened, Brooke noted.

After his confession of the plight of the armies he commanded, Weygand brought up a plan that seemed to point to an unsuspected spirit of resistance. The British and French governments had, he said, decided to defend the peninsula of Brittany with a new, 100-mile front line.

Brooke did not think much of this. Holding the front would require at least fifteen divisions which were simply not available. The Germans dominated the air. In ten days of fighting in France, seventy-five RAF planes had been shot down or destroyed on the ground and another 120 were unserviceable or lacked fuel to fly; in all, the British had lost a quarter of their fighter strength while German planes wreaked havoc with their dive-bombing raids.

Nor, it turned out, did Weygand or his deputy, General Georges, approve of the Brittany idea, though it was said to have caught the fancy of the Deputy Defence Minister, de Gaulle. The French Commander-in-Chief called the notion 'romantic', and said it had been dreamed up by politicians without military advice. But he insisted that they had to follow instructions, and that the British must join in.

Returning to his headquarters on the afternoon of 14 June, Brooke rang the Chief of the Imperial General Staff in London to ask about the Brittany scheme. Dill knew nothing about it, but undertook to ask Churchill.

The unreality in the air was extraordinary. Though Churchill had made his priorities quite plain in the meetings at Briare and Tours, the government in London sent a message to France promising the 'utmost aid in her power'. British newspapers reported enthusiastically about reinforcements being sent across the Channel. They were, said *The Times*, 'well equipped and with high hearts'. Most were Canadians who wore carnations as they embarked in a skirl of bagpipes – the newspaper's reporter noted that one carried a mandolin and another a tin of fruit salad.

After a couple of days in France, Brooke's initial reservations about organising a new BEF to resist the Germans had multiplied. He told Dill that, given the 'general state of disintegration which was setting in to the French Army', all further movement of troops and materiel to France should stop, and arrangements should be started for wholesale evacuation.[22]

An hour later, Dill telephoned back to say that Churchill knew nothing of the Brittany plan – it had been mentioned at his meetings with Reynaud and de Gaulle had expressed interest, but nothing had been agreed. Still, the Prime Minister was anxious that everything should be done to ensure good relations with the French government, which had retreated further south to Bordeaux. Driven by a mixture of pride and realpolitik, Churchill did not want it to appear that Britain was deserting its ally.

Brooke had lost all patience with any such niceties. He had made up his mind that the only thing to do was to save as many troops as possible. Dill said that Churchill did not wish him to do that.

'What the hell does he want?' Brooke responded.

'He wants to speak to you,' Dill said.

The Prime Minister came on the line. He and Brooke spoke for half-an-hour, the General on the verge of losing his temper.

Churchill stressed how important it was to make the French feel they were getting British support.

Brooke replied that it was 'impossible to make a corpse feel'. The French Army, he added, was dead to all intents and purposes. The main priority should be to get as many men back to Britain as possible.

'All right, I agree with you,' Churchill said at last.

So the call went out for ships to join in the final rescue mission from France, and the *Lancastria* set out on her fateful voyage.

CHAPTER 2

Saturday, 15 June 1940

THE BRITISH GARRISON command in St-Nazaire had been told that, if an evacuation was decided, it would receive one of two signals. PIP would mean it should arrange to leave France in twenty-four hours. PIP PIP would mean that it had forty-eight hours. At ten in the morning on 15 June, it picked up the single PIP signal. In his camp, the wireless operator, Mervyn Llewelyn-Jones, noted in his diary: 'June 15. Two letters from my darling. Evacuating, stand by for moving off.'[1]

As the *Lancastria* had sailed through the night to Plymouth, her crew saw other boats following the same course. They could sense that they were part of a big operation from the lights of the ships heading down the west coast or coming out of the Bristol Channel. Following Churchill's telephone conversation with Alan Brooke, vessels were already sailing across the Channel to pick up men from Cherbourg in Normandy, and in Brittany from St Malo and from Brest at the tip of the peninsula.

Few naval craft were to be seen. Nearly all the vessels were merchant ships. Some had once carried fruit from Africa; others had been passenger boats. It hardly looked a fleet constituted to go into battle, particularly not a battle that was being so decisively lost. The crew of one destroyer had been told that the operation was merely 'to embark surplus base personnel'.

While the *Lancastria* waited in Plymouth for sailing orders, naval officials came aboard to inspect the accommodation that would be available for troops being evacuated from France. Chief Officer Harry Grattidge looked up the ridge of the Hoe above the harbour, where Francis Drake had played his famous game of bowls as the Spanish Armada approached. Girls in summer dresses were idling in the summer sun. To Grattidge, they seemed 'almost unreasonably beautiful'.[2]

Across the Channel, advocates of an armistice were increasing the pressure on Premier Paul Reynaud by the hour. Hope of American intervention had been dashed by a message from Roosevelt who expressed moral support, but, because of anti-war sentiment at home, asked that his message should not be made public. In a follow-up message to Churchill, the President made plain that there was no question of being able to commit his country to military involvement, even if he had wished to do so. That was a matter for Congress, and Congress, clearly, would agree to no such thing.

The figurehead of France's peace party, Marshal Pétain, threatened to quit the government unless an armistice was sought. At one point the ancient, white-haired soldier drafted a letter of resignation in protest at the delay in opening negotiations with the Germans. Reynaud changed his mind constantly, badgered by his mistress to end the war: in search of a little rest, he took the line of least resistance with her, telling a friend: 'You don't know what a man who has been hard at work all day will put up with to make sure of an evening's peace.'[3]

After the French Cabinet approved a motion to explore German terms for an armistice, the Premier sent the leading military advocate of resistance, Charles de Gaulle, to London in a final bid to try to get Churchill to provide assistance. Before leaving Bordeaux, the 49-year-old general had dinner at the Hôtel Splendide. Pétain was sitting at the next table. At the end of his meal, de Gaulle went over to shake the Marshal's hands. Neither said anything. It was the last time they met.

Since no plane was available, de Gaulle set out to drive with an aide through the night up the west coast to Brittany where he would take a ship for England. On the way, he called in to see his dying mother, and his wife and two daughters. Reaching Brest, he boarded one of the last naval boats to leave the harbour, the destroyer, *Milan*. Arriving on British soil, he took the train to London where he lodged at the Hyde Park Hotel beside the French embassy.

Far from being ready to send in the men and planes France wanted, the British were concentrating on getting as many as possible back across the Channel. Having won his argument with Churchill, Alan Brooke was intent on saving the maximum number. He had no interest in fighting the enemy or staying in France while guns and supplies were loaded on evacuation ships. The political difficulty, he recorded in his diary, was 'to extract the existing forces without giving the impression that we were abandoning our ally in its hour of need.'[4] Still, his own movements left no doubt about his intentions as he shifted his headquarters each day from Le Mans to Vitré and then to Redon, north of St-Nazaire.

After the losses at Dunkirk, and given its other obligations, the Royal Navy could not spare enough ships to set up a proper convoy system, so the Commander-in-Chief at Portsmouth, Admiral James, decided to run continuous flotillas across the Channel with available warships acting as a screen and providing escorts.

Patriotic feeling was running high, and fishermen all along the south-west coast volunteered to help. There were offers of boats from Brixham, Dartmouth, Exmouth, Falmouth, Fowey, Teignmouth and Torquay. A trawler company in Torbay, which had sent ships to Dunkirk, said it wanted to join in again. 'They arrived faster than we could deal with them,' a naval report recorded.[5] 'Improvisation was the order of the day.' By 15 June, a fleet had been assembled of 50 merchant vessels, 23 destroyers and 20 armed trawlers.

Known as Operation Aerial, the evacuations from the major ports of Normandy and Brittany were strikingly successful. The official British naval history reports that 186,700 British, French and Polish soldiers and airmen were rescued.[6] Some boarded French boats. In one case, men from the Royal Engineers had to brandish a pistol to get the captain to take them; there was so little space on board that they had to abandon their kitbags and their last sight of France was of people on the quayside grabbing the contents.

There was no recorded loss of life in these evacuations from the main ports, and no major damage to vessels. The haste meant, however, that valuable arms and equipment which could have been taken off were left behind. For all the speed of their advance, the Germans were not as close to the north-western coast as the British command believed because of faulty intelligence and the general air of panic gripping France.

Some of the soldiers who had embarked from southern England the previous day never landed in France – their ships were told to return home. The Canadians, who had advanced to Laval in the Mayenne department, were instructed to turn round and head for St-Malo when they were some twenty miles from the German vanguard – their total losses were six men who went missing somewhere in their journey through France. A Canadian colonel commented acidly that the British command appeared to be in 'abject fear' of being overtaken by the Germans. The withdrawal was, he added, 'conducted as a rout'. The official naval historian, Captain Roskill, noted in his account of the war at sea that 'the end was premature'.[7] Still, it saved well over 100,000 men for the defence of Britain against the expected German invasion, and for later service in Europe and the Middle East.

French newspapers were still printing official communiqués reporting that the defenders were inflicting heavy casualties on the Wehrmacht in the east, but nobody believed them any more. German planes dominated the skies and Panzer units forged at will across the country. Though there were instances of resistance – at Tours, 300 North African troops held up the Germans for three days in a battle that set the city on fire – the Maginot Line had been pierced and the enemy took the highly symbolic First World War strong point of Verdun. Rather than flying into battle, French planes were being towed on long trailers to the south-west. The 'certain eventuality' envisaged after Dunkirk was fast becoming reality.

In the early stages of Operation Aerial, 84,700 men were taken off by evacuation ships from Brest, Cherbourg and St-Malo. Another 21,300 were rescued from smaller ports. That left almost 50,000 men in the far west of France round Nantes and St-Nazaire at the mouth of the River Loire. Meeting an hour after receiving the PIP signal, the officers of the St-Nazaire garrison drew up plans to ship them to safety on the evacuation flotilla that would be making its way round the Brittany peninsula from southern England.

A captain from the garrison went into the town to make arrangements to withdraw the remains of 80 million francs the British had deposited at the Banque de France office to cover their expenditure. A young woman member of the bank staff called Denise Petit remembered him as having been 'so refined, delicate, thoroughbred'.

'What will happen to us, Captain, with the Germans?' she asked.

'Don't despair,' he replied. 'We will be back. Sometimes England loses the first round, sometimes even the second one, but never the third one.'

He gave Denise a small photograph with his signature. Two

days later, the Captain boarded the *Lancastria*, and was believed to have been among those who died.

Troops from inland began to get to St-Nazaire on 15 June. Denise Petit watched them 'arriving from all sides, abandoning their supplies and equipment'. Most were directed to a half-finished airfield outside the town. Many more were still on their way across western France under the summer sun.

As they abandoned their bases, the British broke up and burned equipment, vehicles and stores to prevent them falling into German hands. Some fitted themselves with new boots from abandoned army stores for the trek to the sea. They slept in fields or village squares. One artillery unit, which had come all the way from Champagne, was woken during the night by a town crier announcing that Paris was surrounded: the soldiers got to their feet and hurried on. Another unit passed a travelling circus, led by six elephants ridden by mahouts. Heading west by train, Sherwood Foresters found the track cut by bombs. They repaired the line and, when the driver refused to go on, persuaded him to change his mind by sticking a pistol in his ribs. Moving more slowly on foot from Rouen, other Foresters stopped from time to time to play housey-housey with their remaining francs.

'Cobber' Kain's unit, the 73rd squadron of the RAF, was among those moving west. Instead of joining the retreat, wireless operator Vic Flowers, who had been in the crowd that watched the ace plunge to his death, volunteered to go to a base from which planes were still due to fly against the Germans. An officer ordered him to take the place of a wounded air gunner on a Fairey Battle bomber waiting to take off. Flowers said he had never been up in an aircraft and had no idea how to fire a machine gun. The officer insisted that he get in, but Flowers managed to disappear from the scene though, as he later recalled, 'the penalties for failing to comply with an order on the field of battle were very severe'.

He got a ride on a lorry to another airfield where he was put to work unloading hundreds of four-gallon tins of high octane fuel from a wagon which caught fire as the last few cans were being taken off. On 15 June, Flowers and other men from ground crews were told to board available trucks, and make for Nantes. On the way, they passed airfields with rows of burned out Battle and Blenheim bombers. Arriving at Le Mans, they were taken aback to see NAAFI stores deserted; everyone was helping themselves to cigarettes and tobacco from wooden crates that had been broken open. Five hundred motorcycles had been stored at the British camp on the city's racetrack, and RAF ground crews were riding them round for fun.

Edwin Quittenton of the Royal Engineers had a particularly erratic journey across France. Originally, he and a colleague had been ordered to drive a five-ton lorry from Abbeville to Reims in Champagne, 130 miles to the east. Their mission was to bring back stores and provisions from an abandoned depot. On the way they passed through deserted towns bereft of any sign of life – not even a cat or dog.

At the depot, they spent two hours loading the lorry with tinned food, cases of cigarettes and whisky and wines. They ate, smoked and drank, and then decided it was time to head back to Abbeville.

Suddenly they heard the sound of bullets. Looking out of

the driver's cab, they saw German planes diving on the depot. 'Blimey, Jerry's here,' they shouted at one another.

Speeding off, they took corners on two wheels, and did not stop until they reached a British army barricade thirty miles down the road. The sides and the back of the lorry were riddled by bullets. All the bottles of whisky had been hit. The tins of fruit were holed, and the juice inside had run out. Only the cigarettes had escaped damage.

Getting back to Abbeville, Quittenton endured a big bombing raid before driving across Normandy to Rouen to join a group of Royal Engineers that had been told to impede the German advance and destroy supplies and oil tanks. But the enemy advance was too strong, and he followed a crazy pattern across northern France, dodging back to Le Havre, and then driving 300 miles to Nantes before doubling back with his comrades to try to find an evacuation ship at Cherbourg. No luck there, so they went down to Granville at the bottom of the Cotentin peninsula. No luck there, either, so they drove across to Rennes. A brief stay there as German planes staged bombing raids. Then back to Nantes where Quittenton became the driver for a commanding officer he described as 'a thorough gentleman'.

Captain Griggs of the Royal Engineers, who would swim through dead fish in his full uniform and tin helmet, found a blue Vauxhall saloon car in a ditch and recruited a French driver to take him along the Normandy coast from his base at Le Tréport to Dieppe. Then he went south-west, enjoying a good lunch, stopping at bistros along the way to sample their wares, and spending the night at a 'very pleasant Pension'.

Heading the same way, Sergeant Macpherson of the RAF, dozed in the armchair in the back of the lorry that had brought him from Olivet. After Nantes, he and his companions drove on for forty miles to a base outside St-Nazaire. There, a squadron leader ordered all the available food – corned beef, potatoes, cheese and baked beans – to be put into a massive pot, covered with water and condiments, stirred and boiled furiously for an hour. 'Curiously,' Macpherson recalled, 'it was not such a bad mess, and everybody had some.'

Some of those seeking a way out of France made their own way to the evacuation ports, or found themselves unexpectedly exposed to the enemy. A British teacher, Grace Classey, who had been on the staff of a school in France for five years, hitched rides through Brittany to join a ship taking soldiers home.

Margaret Ellis, an army nurse stationed at Offranville, near Dieppe, was woken early one morning by her matron and told to get dressed and to leave immediately, without stopping to pack. Ellis grabbed a few essentials, including a quarter-pound packet of tea. Rather than going to Dieppe, which was under heavy bombing, she and her colleagues headed south-west, without food and sleeping in barns and haystacks. When they arrived in Le Mans, British officers offered them dinner at their hotel, and gave up their rooms though there were not enough beds – Ellis slept on the floor. The town was bombed during the night. The next day, they boarded a train for the coast. There, they found a rescue ship and set off on an eighteen-hour voyage across the Channel, using water heated in the engine-room boiler to make themselves tea.

A group of Canadian soldiers was taken by train from the

coast down to Tours, unaware that the Germans were encircling the city on the Loire. When they arrived, a British officer told them of the military situation. The Canadians tried to get the engine driver to take them back to the coast. He refused to budge. So four of them worked out how the locomotive was operated, and set off for the north, the others poking their rifles through the open windows. They made it to the Channel, and found places on a boat.

One of the more extraordinary individual escapes was made by a trio of soldiers headed by a corporal called Patrick Hanley, from Deal in Kent. At the beginning of June, their unit had been posted to block a road to the coast. They suddenly found themselves faced with a German armoured convoy that stretched back for ten miles. When the order 'Every man for himself' was given, Hanley hid in a wood for the night with two privates. In the morning, they were discovered by the Germans, and locked in a church. After eight days there, Hanley told the others that he had had enough, and would 'clout' the guard when he came round in the evening. He duly did this; so the three of them escaped, hiding in another wood for four days with no nourishment except for milk they took from a cow. Then they sheltered in a barn where a farmer found them, and gave them food.

Setting out again, the trio met a group of Belgian refugees who handed them civilian clothes. Stealing bicycles, they headed for the coast, but were stopped by German troops, and taken to the commander. Hanley said they were Belgian, though he had no papers. The German officer, who did not speak French, believed him. So they got away again, reaching the Channel coast. There, they pretended to be beachcombers, rolling up their trousers and walking about with seaweed draped over their shoulders while they decided what to do next.

Two girls they ran into told them of a rowing boat abandoned in a garage by a doctor who had joined the refugee exodus. The boat was white, which the soldiers thought too conspicuous. So they got hold of some black paint, and used it to darken the craft. The girls gave them food to take with them, as well as a Union Jack and corks with which to plug holes from machine-gunning if they were strafed. Rowing through the night, they became extremely seasick, but got home in the end.

In Nantes, Major Fred Hahn, the First World War veteran from Lancashire who had passed his time watching tennis and meeting local Masons, was put in charge of ensuring food supplies for the British troops camped on the racecourse, where French recruits practised driving two-men Hotchkiss tanks.

It was a tough assignment because rations were non-existent. Bread was scarce. What provisions Hahn could find were old and mouldy. Stores had been abandoned and, in some cases, looted. The Major was more in his element when he and a few others were given the job of salvaging equipment, including secret radar parts, after the main body of troops moved off to St-Nazaire. Guards with Bren guns were posted round the workshop as Hahn went to work dismantling equipment and loading it on to lorries.

Another transport detachment posted behind a network of trenches outside Nantes had got an idea of the way things were going when its women ATS staff had been taken back to Britain on 12 June. In their absence, the men found office work extremely difficult. As a defence against the Germans, they stretched steel wire at a 45 degree angle across nearby roads: they reckoned it could pitch a light tank into the ditch. They also formed a 'flying column' of a truck mounted with a Bren gun and two lorries carrying twenty men each to deal with any German parachutists who might drop on them.

At 1 p.m. on 15 June, the men were called to the parade ground to be told they would be leaving. They began to pack up their machine tools and stores, and to dismantle big pieces of equipment. French civilians working at the base were sent to remote parts of the facility so that they should not see what was going on. At 6 p.m., the first convoy left for St-Nazaire with lathes and drilling machines.

Lieutenant Colonel Norman de Coudray Tronson, the 64-year-old Boer War veteran who would fire a Bren gun at the attacking planes from the deck of the *Lancastria*, reached the end of his exodus across France in La Baule. He had fought in India and South Africa as well as in the First World War when he was gassed and wounded. He had been sent to Dieppe to supervise hospital facilities and a medical depot. The Norman port became the target of heavy raids by German aircraft whose crews took no notice of the big red crosses painted on the roofs of medical centres. The house where Tronson was staying was hit three times, destroying most of his possessions. Two British hospital ships were bombed. One, the *Maid of Kent*, keeled over, and set fire to a train drawn up alongside containing 580 wounded men. The planes came back, and began machine-gunning. 'That's when the real horror began,' said an army major at the scene.

After the raid, Tronson sent medical stores to the west, and then left at the head of a convoy of six cars at midnight. In the morning, he stopped in the town of Alençon, in southern Normandy, for breakfast and a haircut. There was no sign of the other five cars, but he did not wait. On the way west, he met up with a train carrying members of his staff from Dieppe. They headed for La Baule, with its luxury hotels behind the wide, three-mile-long beach converted into military hospitals to treat men brought in from across northern France. When the evacuation order was transmitted on 15 June dozen of military ambulances lined up outside to carry the wounded to St-Nazaire.

Some of the retreating foreigners did not behave so well. One British soldier carried a valise crammed with leather shoe soles; another filled his map pocket with hundred franc notes he collected along the way. A sergeant carried two haversacks stuffed with clocks, watches and other souvenirs of France. A driver known as 'Matey', with a headquarters unit of the Royal Engineers, made off with an album of beautifully drawn and coloured pornographic illustrations he came across. After showing them round, he tucked them into his uniform jacket to take home. They would go down with him on the *Lancastria*.

In Nantes, a newspaper reported an incident at a farmhouse in the region. Two foreign soldiers had asked the farmer's wife for food, which she gave them. As they were eating, a delivery man arrived with a package. To pay him, the woman went to a cupboard to get money stored there. The next day, while she was out, the money was stolen, along with savings books kept in the cupboard. The report left no doubt that it was the foreign soldiers who were responsible. Whether they were British was not specified.

A handful of civilians were also trying to get out through St-Nazaire. Among them were members of the YMCA and the Church Army – a convoy carrying two of its sisters called Trott and Chamley was attacked five times by German planes.

In La Baule, an Englishwoman from London, Mrs Jory, had stayed on with three of her children in their family villa on the calculation that London might be bombed and that a resort in western France would be safer. As she watched the army ambulances lining up outside the hotel-hospitals to take the wounded to be evacuated, she realised that it was time to go. She got a pass for the *Lancastria*, but did not manage to obtain one for her young sons and daughter. The family's large Austin car did not have enough petrol to drive to St-Nazaire. So the family stayed in La Baule, and the children stood on the beach watching German planes flying in to bomb the ships in the bay – at the end of 1940, they were arrested by the Germans and the French police, and held in several camps before being freed in 1944.

Most of the civilians who did get to St-Nazaire came from an aircraft factory operated by the Fairey Aviation Company near Charleroi in Belgium. The plant had been bombed at the start of the German offensive in May, and the firm decided to evacuate its management and their families to France. With them, they carried plans for aircraft construction that the British did not want to fall into enemy hands.

Among those in the Fairey party were 13-year-old Emilie Legroux and her brother, Roger, eleven, three-year-old

Claudine Freeman and a baby, Jacqueline Tillyer, aged two. The women and children set off by car, the men by tram.

They found a train that took them across the French border to Valenciennes where it was stopped by a heavy bombing raid – the men lay on top of the children to protect them. After the planes had gone, the children complained loudly about having been crushed. One of the mothers knocked their heads together, telling them, 'We have enough wars as it is.'

Another train got them to within twenty miles of Paris, but it stopped there, and the party spent the night in a field. In the morning, they boarded another train thinking it was for the French capital. Instead, it went south, and they ended up near Bordeaux, where they moved into an inn that offered baths as well as food.

From there, they contacted the Fairey head office in Hayes, Middlesex, and were instructed to get to England. So they made their way up the west coast of France by rail to find a route to Britain.

As the Fairey group was heading for Nantes and St-Nazaire, the Kampfgeschwader 30 (KG30) unit of the Luftwaffe was settling into its new base outside Louvain, east of Brussels. It had been allocated an abandoned airfield that was little more than a harvested field from which to mount sorties against France.

Kampfgeschwader 30 was an elite group, flying the new Junkers JU-88 bombers, with the unit's symbol of a diving eagle emblazoned on their noses. The twin-engined planes were among the most destructive and frightening elements in the Nazi attack, diving at almost 300 miles an hour to release their bombs as their siren hooters set up a banshee wail to frighten people below.

No sooner had they arrived in Belgium than the Diving Eagles were sent to attack France. On the way, they landed to take on fuel at an abandoned RAF airfield outside Amiens where one of the Germans found a big box of English sweets left behind by the retreating airmen. From Amiens, the JU-88s flew west, diving through anti-aircraft fire to attack the port at Cherbourg from which British troops were being evacuated. One of the fliers, a newly married, former civilian test pilot called Peter Stahl, was struck by the desolation below him on the way. He noted the numbers of cows lying dead in the fields, and the crush of people on the roads.

The Diving Eagles did not attack the refugees; that was a job for smaller aircraft. They were after larger prey, strategic bridges, communications points and ships – one of their main training exercises had been to swoop on an old battleship to gain experience of attacking big naval targets.

At 9.30 in the evening of 15 June, Winston Churchill's private secretary, John Colville, told him the latest bad news from France as they went in to dinner at the Prime Minister's official residence at Chequers in Buckinghamshire. Churchill became very depressed, so the meal began in a lugubrious atmosphere. The Prime Minister ate quickly and greedily, his face almost down in the plate. As well as Colville, his scientific adviser, Professor Frederick Lindeman, was present, eating a special vegetarian menu. The Prime Minister's eldest daughter, Diana, and her husband, the politician, Duncan Sandys, completed the party.

Champagne, brandy and cigars lightened Churchill's mood, and the group became talkative, 'even garrulous', Colville recorded in his diary.[8]

'The war is bound to become a bloody one for us now,' the Prime Minister said. 'But our people will stand up to bombing.' He was particularly concerned that, if France gave up, its fleet should not fall into German hands. 'If they let us have their fleet we shall never forget, but . . . if they surrender without consulting us, we shall never forgive,' he declared. 'We shall blacken their name for a thousand years.'

Churchill and Sandys stepped into the garden, walking in the moonlight as they discussed the latest events. In the distance, sentries with fixed bayonets watched over them.

Returning to the house, Churchill recited some poetry, and said he and Hitler had only one thing in common, their hatred of whistling. Then he began to murmur:

> *Bang, Bang, Bang goes the farmer's gun,*
> *Run, rabbit, run rabbit, run, run, run.*

The American ambassador, Joseph Kennedy, telephoned, and Colville heard Churchill speaking forcefully about how the United States could save civilisation.

By then, Captain Sharp had received his sailing orders in Plymouth, and the *Lancastria* was heading for France in the company of another big liner, the *Franconia*, which had been the flagship of the evacuation fleet from Norway.

As they set their course across the western end of the Channel, the Prime Minister lay on a sofa and told dirty stories while his guests stood in the central hallway of the house listening. At 1.30 a.m., he got to his feet. 'Goodnight, my children,' he said as he went up the stairs to bed.

While Churchill slept in Buckinghamshire, the *Lancastria* steamed towards Brest to take off British troops. Nobody knew how many men would be waiting, but, to make sure the soldiers would be fed on the voyage back, the ship's bakery set to work making as much bread as possible.

CHAPTER 3

Sunday, 16 June 1940

APPROACHING THE FORTIFIED PORT and naval centre of Brest on the Brittany peninsula, the *Lancastria*'s crew saw great columns of smoke rising into the sky from oil tanks set on fire to prevent the fuel being used by the Germans when they arrived. Chief Officer Harry Grattidge described the pall as looking like rich black velvet. French troops formed two defensive lines outside the fortified city, but the burning of the fuel dumps showed how little confidence the defenders had in holding their positions.

Nine hundred tons of gold bullion from the Bank of France was being put on ships to be taken to safety in colonial possessions in Africa. The *Strathaird*, a former P&O liner converted into a troopship, was loading men; she would sail home with 6500 the next day.

Luftwaffe dive bombers had just attacked a French cruiser, the *Richelieu*, moored in the harbour, without, however, scoring any hits. They also dropped magnetic mines in the roads leading to the harbour. Given the danger, Captain Sharp decided not to try to sail the *Lancastria* into Brest; instead, he set a southerly course down the coast towards the Bay of Quiberon. The Canadian helmsman, Michael Sheehan, heard him say they were heading for St-Nazaire.

The *Franconia*, the other big liner which had left Plymouth the previous day, accompanied the *Lancastria*. A destroyer, HMS *Wolverine*, on patrol duty outside Brest, acted as escort, and a French trawler guided them through the twisting channels between the Quiberon peninsula and the island of Belle Île, some 100 miles south of Brest.

Suddenly, a German plane came screaming out of the hazy sky. Sheehan heard the noise of machine-gunning. Then there was silence for an hour. After that, German planes returned to drop bombs between the two liners, sending up a white jet of water. Neither ship was hit, but the force of the explosions was so great that one of the *Franconia*'s engines was knocked out of line and her plates were so badly buckled that she risked becoming unseaworthy. So, her captain decided to stop to make what repairs he could on the spot, and then limped back to England: water was washing over the *Franconia*'s footplates when she pulled into Liverpool.

The *Wolverine* returned to her patrol station off Brest, leaving the *Lancastria* alone. The skipper of a passing French trawler warned Sharp that the Luftwaffe had been conducting heavy raids in the bay. In the distance, a convoy of seven British merchant ships from South Wales came into sight, sailing in single file, led by the *John Holt*, from the Blue Funnel line, which specialised in carrying fruit from Africa. On board was an admiral who acted as naval commodore.

Under thick clouds, the convoy was heading at full speed for St-Nazaire. As night fell, Sharp joined it.

At St-Etienne-de-Montluc, outside Nantes, the men of the Number One Heavy Repair Shop were called on to the parade ground as usual in the morning of 16 June. But, this time, they received new orders; they were to head home, though not quite yet. There was still no sense of urgency. It was only later in the day that they began to smash up vehicles and equipment, disabling engines, breaking axles and slashing tyres. The chimney of a porcelain factory they had used as a workshop was brought down by the Royal Engineers, the debris strewn across a railway track. A diesel engine was run into buffers at full speed to wreck it.

Stan Flowers took a big hammer to a machine he had much prized, a big crankshaft grinder which had been brought to St-Etienne and bedded down in concrete to repair vehicles. What he was doing broke his heart. But he got on with the job, and then climbed into the cab of a lorry to cause as much damage as he could there, too. Behind the driver's seat was a plaque reading:

> *Look after me and keep me well,*
> *And together we will serve our country and we will*
> *survive.*

After reading the words, Stan smashed it.

He and his colleagues burned their kit in the field which housed their latrines. They would have preferred to have left their gear for the French inhabitants of the town who had been so friendly. But orders were orders. The burning completed, they formed up and set off in trucks for the coast. As they went, French people stood along the street, crying. The soldiers were watchful as they moved off, having heard rumours of Germans dressed in British uniforms sending convoys the wrong way. When planes swooped on them, several jumped from the lorries into a roadside cesspit for shelter.

As the day drew on, the crush of men moving into St-Nazaire grew by the hour. Most came along the hedge-lined road from Nantes, across flat countryside past one-storey farmhouses and tall steepled churches. Outside the port, they were directed to the half-completed airfield, which was being used as a rallying point. The traffic was so dense that progress was very slow.

Conditions soon became chaotic under the weight of numbers flooding in. Some of the men were accompanied by French girls wheeling bicycles. Others dropped by a NAAFI store that had been opened up, and took what they pleased – Stan Flowers grabbed a pair of sports shoes, only discovering later that they were for the same foot.

An RAF officer, Wing Commander Macfadyen, estimated that 10,000 men were milling around. They would have been sitting targets for German bombers, but no enemy planes appeared. Macfadyen's unit of nine officers and 210 men found itself caught up in a three-mile traffic jam as it moved from Nantes towards the airfield. Others abandoned their lorries to make progress on foot through the throng. At the wheel of his Humber Snipe staff car, Joe Sweeney edged through the crowd. When he reached the airfield, a French civilian thrust 5000 francs into his hand, got into the car and drove it away – he was stopped at the gate by a military policeman, taken out of the car and handed over to the French police.

At the airfield, there were no orders. When Macfadyen grew annoyed at this, he was told he could head for the harbour. The scene there was equally confused, with men packed tightly together as they inched forward to French tenders that would take them to ships moored in the estuary. The queue in front of Macfadyen stretched for at least half a mile along the quay.

Captain Clem Stott, the accountant from Wales who would use his army boots to kick himself free of a man threatening to drag him under the water, got to St-Nazaire with his fifty-strong Pay Corps unit during the afternoon of 16 June. Exhausted, filthy and hungry, they were given tins of fruit and chocolate bars from the NAAFI. Behind them, a detachment of RAF men arrived, looking as fresh and smart as if they were on parade.

Another Pay Corps unit stationed near the coast was told to form up in full marching order outside the town hall after breakfast that morning. Their commanding officer told them that the Germans were approaching, and that the local Mayor had said they had to leave within an hour. So he ordered them to set off towards St-Nazaire. They had not been told of the evacuation, and simply hoped they would be able to pick up a boat to get home.

Suddenly there was a shout of 'Take cover!' The soldiers dived into ditches as a German plane flew over very low. But it did not fire. A little while later, the same shout went up, and the plane flew over once more, again not firing. It must have been on a reconnaissance mission.

*

In Britain, that Sunday had been declared a day of prayer for France. At his official country residence, Churchill lay in bed, reading the latest news of war developments brought by a dispatch rider from London. The Prime Minister's secretary, John Colville, thought he looked 'just like a rather nice pig clad in a silk vest'.[1] Having finished the reports, Churchill ruminated for a while before deciding to return to London and call a Cabinet meeting for 10.30. There, it was decided to tell the French that they could investigate German armistice terms on condition that their fleet immediately set sail for British harbours. Without the fleet, Britain would continue to hold Paul Reynaud to the agreement not to seek a separate peace.

As Churchill was reading the latest news in bed at Chequers, the French ambassador, Charles Corbin, was on his way to the Hyde Park Hotel with an eminent French international official and banker, Jean Monnet, who had been sent to try to use his contacts in London to get reinforcements for France. The previous day, over lunch at the Conservative Party stronghold of the Carlton Club, Corbin had discussed an audacious idea with the Foreign Secretary, Lord Halifax, and other high British figures. What evolved was the notion of forming a union between their two countries as a means of keeping France in the war. On Sunday morning, Corbin and Monnet decided to put the scheme to Charles de Gaulle.

The future leader of the Free French was shaving when two visitors called. Monnet spoke of the value of binding Britain and France together in a political, military and economic union. Though the difficulties of the scheme were evident, de Gaulle agreed. So did other French officials in London who were consulted.

De Gaulle was already showing the mettle and bravado that would mark his long career. Despite having no authority to do so, he had just issued an order for a French merchant ship loaded with arms and ammunition to put into a British port rather than sailing to his country's occupied northern coast. Shortly after noon, the General telephoned Paul Reynaud in Bordeaux to tell him that 'something stupendous' was being prepared. Though the British government had not yet formally considered the idea, de Gaulle said bluntly that 'Churchill proposes the establishment of a single Franco-British government'.[2] Then he added a most unlikely carrot, suggesting that Reynaud might become head of a joint War Cabinet. Having set the ball rolling, he went to meet Churchill for lunch at the Carlton Club.

At 3 p.m., the War Cabinet met in Whitehall to discuss the proposal. After harbouring initial doubts, Churchill concluded that 'some dramatic announcement was clearly necessary to keep the French going'. De Gaulle and Corbin sat outside the Cabinet Room, officials coming out from time to time to consult them. At 4 p.m., the General made another telephone call to Reynaud to say that there was going to be 'a sensational declaration'. The French Premier warned that he must have it before his Cabinet met that evening if he was to head off the defeatists.

After two hours of discussion, the War Cabinet approved a declaration that France and Great Britain 'shall no longer be two nations but one Franco-British Union'. The two countries, it said, were joined indissolubly in their 'unyielding resolution in their common defence of justice and freedom, against subjection to a system which reduces mankind to a life of robots and slaves'. They would have joint defence, foreign, financial and economic policy organs, and a single War

Cabinet during the conflict in charge of all their forces. The two parliaments would be formally associated. And thus, the declaration concluded: 'We shall conquer.'

It was an amazing leap of faith for a government which included its fair share of hard-headed realists, and a sign of how desperate the situation had become. Despite having flirted at one point with the idea of trying to open negotiations with Hitler, Lord Halifax backed the scheme. So did the two Labour Party members of the Cabinet, Clement Attlee and Arthur Greenwood. On the French side, his later unshakable defence of French sovereignty gave an ironic tinge to de Gaulle's involvement though, as the future 'Father of Europe' and promoter of the original Common Market, Jean Monnet was acting entirely in character.

'*Nous sommes d'accord,*' Churchill cried as he emerged from the Cabinet Room, launching into an impromptu speech while ministers clapped de Gaulle on the back and told him he would become Commander-in-Chief. '*Je l'arrangerai,*' Churchill broke in. The Prime Minister's private secretary wondered if the General was a new Napoleon. 'From what I hear, it seems a lot of people think so,' Colville added in his diary.[3] 'He treats Reynaud (whom he called *ce poisson gelé*) like dirt.' What nobody in London seems to have taken into account was the danger that the proposal would make those in Bordeaux intent on reaching an armistice even more determined to take the final steps to end France's war.

Heading for evacuation from St-Nazaire, Horace Lumsden heard news of the unity proposal on the radio. He and his fellow soldiers approved, but they realised they were caught up in 'a major disaster'. What particularly struck Lumsden was the blank expression on the faces of the French people crowding the roads. It was, he thought, as if they did not understand what was going on and, if they did, could not grasp it.

When he arrived at the airfield outside St-Nazaire, Lance Corporal Morris Lashbrook and his friend, Alan 'Chippy' Moore, scouted round to see the lie of the land. They were both very hungry after the drive from St-Etienne-de-Montluc. They found a field kitchen, and plenty of wood. The only food to hand was bully beef, potatoes and margarine. They cooked it up, and helped the meal down with Scotch from a bottle provided by one of their officers. Then they were ordered to set out on foot for the docks.

Feeling bored in a Royal Engineers camp some thirty miles from the coast, Neville Chesterton, the former railway clerk from Staffordshire whose unit had wandered apparently aimlessly across France, decided to go to a cinema in a local town with a friend called Derek. They thought the trip would pass the time though neither would understand the French dialogue.

They were let into the cinema without paying. There were only half a dozen other people inside. As the film went on, Chesterton and Derek heard excited chattering round them, and the audience began to slip out. By the time the film had finished, the hall was empty. The French had left after hearing rumours that their government had surrendered.

*

British troops in St-Nazaire began to embark on the first evacuation boats that had arrived during the afternoon of 16 June. Two big troopships, the *Georgic* and the *Duchess of York*, lay well off the coast in Quiberon Bay together with two Polish vessels, the *Batory* and the *Sobieski*. They had no protection against German planes or submarines, but were not attacked. In St-Nazaire, a hospital ship pulled into the harbour and, shouting through a megaphone, the captain offered to take men on board if they left their weapons behind to enable the boat to keep its noncombatant status – their commanders refused.

Some of the rescue ships had sailed in haste without time to prepare. One was so short of food that the captain and crew went ashore to grab a wooden case that had been dumped on the quayside – it turned out to contain only biscuits. Wanting something more varied, the officers put up 400 francs, and two of them went to buy oranges, potatoes and carrots.

Most of the men on the quays concentrated on getting on to a ship, abandoning their equipment. Noticing cases loaded on lorries left on the docks, the commander of a unit of the 6th Royal Sussex regiment ordered them to be opened. Inside were Bren guns in mint condition, along with ammunition. The officer told his men to grab as many as they could, and they used them subsequently to fire from their rescue ship at attacking German planes.

The weather was balmy. 'The sea is calm and blue, singing on her way to break on the golden shore,' wrote a local newspaper, the *Courrier de St-Nazaire et de la Région*.[4] 'The summer's gentle wind carries with it the perfume of the flowers.'

But the mass of soldiers on the boulevard by the sea acted

as an unwelcome reminder of the reality of war. 'Why this deployment of British forces here?' the newspaper asked. 'It is said that our allies are going back to England. We don't want to believe it and yet, it is true.' It went on:

> On the open sea, big boats are at anchor, waiting for the order to enter the harbour. The presence of these soldiers and boats, which already has brought upon us the nocturnal visits of the German planes, is again going to attract them, day and night in our skies.
>
> A little before midday, we perceive the distant noise of an airplane, and immediately afterwards, the tragic screeching of the sirens pierces the quiet air. Everybody rushes towards the nearest shelter.

The sounding of the all clear meant that people could go home safely through the streets to lunch. But, at about 4 p.m., a lone German aircraft flew over slowly at low altitude. British soldiers strolling on the boulevard threw themselves to the ground as a small round white cloud rose from the ground where the plane's bombs had landed.

'The British are boarding!' a local woman noted in a memoir for her sister, who was in England.

> They fill the whole boulevard, assembled by companies and regiments. It is hot, the weather is close and stormy; they are thirsty. The German planes are above us.
>
> During mass, the air-raid sirens ring out. I am coming back via the boulevard but, to avoid the projectiles, I have to rush under a big porch near the rue Fernand Gasnier. Many British soldiers have also taken refuge there.
>
> This day has been most painful and harrowing. You

can guess our feelings of helplessness and abandonment; it was terrible, and these rumours of a separate armistice which were causing the departure of the English, what a disgrace!

A British doctor who had taken a bedroom in her house came to say farewell on the Sunday evening. 'Mummy and I were crying. We were so sad. But the doctor tried to cheer us up. "We will be back," he said. "All is not lost." Yet I had a foreboding of all the sufferings we would have to endure, of how long and hard the struggle was going to be and of the numerous pitfalls and stumbling blocks that would face us. Would we ever see happier times again?'[5]

In Nantes, the British manager of a wood factory which had made panelling for Atlantic liners was driving back from his plant when German planes flew in to bomb the city. Alfred Edwin Duggan, a First World War veteran, had lived in Nantes since 1920, though he kept up his English habits down to porridge at breakfast. Now, he drove to the British club to see if there was any information there about what was happening. The building was virtually empty; a padre told him British troops had been instructed to evacuate.

Duggan went on to the British consulate where he barged into a meeting between the Consul and the Port Admiral. He insisted on being told what was going on. A British naval attaché advised him to head immediately for St-Nazaire and the rescue fleet waiting there.

Going to his home in the rue de Rennes in the north of the city, Duggan told his wife, his 15-year-old daughter and his 13-year-old son to pack. They filled four suitcases, numbered

1 to 4 – the last, carried by the youngest member of the family, John, was to be abandoned first, if necessary.

Duggan telephoned other British inhabitants of Nantes, only to find that some had already left. Two families joined the Duggans in a three-car convoy which headed towards St-Nazaire. Before setting out, they agreed that, if any car broke down, it would be abandoned. The vital thing was to get to the coast and sail away.

It was, John Duggan recalled, an exciting episode for a teenage boy. The weather was beautiful. He had with him his Bedlington terrier of which he was particularly fond. The road was clogged, and, as they passed through French villages, people cheered them.

The route west from Nantes divides at the town of Savenay, one fork going to St-Nazaire and the other north-west towards Brest. Eddie Duggan looked up the right-hand fork and saw the road was empty. So he decided to take it, giving up the idea of going to St-Nazaire and heading instead for Brest.

One car's fan belt gave way as they passed through a deserted village, where the road became a hard, dusty track. Ignoring their agreement to abandon any vehicle that broke down, the men forced open garages to find a replacement. As they did so, they kept a watch on the road, half expecting to see German tanks driving towards them. John Duggan stood by a water trough, with his terrier. Behind him, he heard a skylark.

German planes were attacking at will across France. The last RAF units had been withdrawn to the Channel Islands. The French air force was largely ineffective.

From the base outside Louvain in Belgium, the KG30 Diving Eagle unit of JU-88s was ordered to bomb Tours. Though the government had left for the greater safety of Bordeaux, the city was still a major point on the refugee route.

Using their usual tactic of flying in with the sun behind them to blind the defenders, the planes dived on a bridge crossing the river. The pilot, Peter Stahl, waited until a red mark on the Plexiglas panel in the nose passed the target. Then he pulled the level that sent his plane into its steep dive. As he hurtled down, an anti-aircraft shell hit the panel, and Stahl pulled the plane upwards. Regaining height, he put the Junkers into a second dive, and, this time, hit the bridge – a few days later, the damage was to prove a hindrance to Wehrmacht troops as they came to cross the Loire.

Back in Belgium, the crews had what Stahl's diary called 'a good serious drinking session with many speeches in the nearby village. The wine is good and our hosts in the local inn are most pleasant.'[6]

France's new capital of Bordeaux was crammed with half a million refugees. People clamoured for rooms in the lobbies of smart hotels, or slept in private homes that were turned into dormitories. The correspondent of *The Times* described the city as being in 'bedlam', with 'ladies bent on saving their lapdogs, refugees of all kinds, French and foreigners [and] a ceaseless maelstrom of cars'.[7]

Government leaders set up in official buildings: Paul Reynaud chose the military commander's residence as a sign of his intention to keep a grip on the conduct of the war. In the late afternoon of 16 June, Churchill's military liaison officer, General Edward Spears, and the British ambassador, Sir Ronald Campbell, called on the Premier with a message from London saying that, if France did seek armistice terms, Britain expected to be consulted.

Then the telephone rang. Reynaud picked up the receiver. The next moment, Spears recorded, 'his eyebrows went up so far they became indistinguishable from his neatly brushed hair; one eyebrow to each side of the parting'.[8]

'One moment,' the Premier said. 'I must take it down.'

The caller was de Gaulle with the terms of the British declaration on union between the two countries.

Grasping a sheet of foolscap paper on the table in front of him, Reynaud began to write in a scrawl, using a short gold pencil with an enormous lead. He repeated each word as he went along, getting more and more excited. Spears held the paper to stop it sliding across the slippery surface. As each sheet was filled, the General handed Reynaud a new one. The Premier's pencil gave out, so the British general handed him his.

Finally, Reynaud said into the mouthpiece, 'Does he agree to this? Did Churchill give you this personally?'

There was a moment's pause. Then Churchill came on the line.

Reynaud started to speak in English. He pledged to defend the union proposal to the death. He would take the appeasers by surprise at the Cabinet meeting that evening. As Spears gathered up the scrawled sheets to carry them to secretaries in the next room to be typed, he glimpsed Reynaud's face 'transfigured with joy . . . happy with a great happiness in the belief that France would now remain in the war'.

The two Prime Ministers agreed to meet the following day in the Breton port of Concarneau. To mark the historic nature of what was happening, Churchill decided to take the senior figures from the Labour and Liberal parties with him, as well as the Chiefs of Staff. He also dropped the demand for the French fleet to sail to British harbours.

Still, the Prime Minister rebuffed a final appeal by de Gaulle to send troops to France: the union had not yet taken shape, and he was not going to abandon his policy of harbouring reserves to defend Britain. A report from a British general on the spot said that the Tenth Army in northern France was in full retreat. Any forces sent across the Channel might well be chewed up by the Wehrmacht. According to Churchill's account, de Gaulle paused as he left the room, took a couple of steps back and said, in English, 'I think you are quite right.' Then he boarded a plane to fly to Bordeaux with the text of the unity declaration.

What neither Churchill nor Reynaud nor de Gaulle knew was that the French Premier's telephone was being tapped – by agents working for France's Commander-in-Chief. They had recorded de Gaulle's call at noon, and his subsequent conversation with Reynaud at 4 p.m. They also noted a call the Premier made at 4.40 p.m. to President Lebrun asking for a private meeting before the Cabinet session.

That was not all. When Spears took the scrawled sheets to be typed up, Reynaud's mistress, Hélène de Portes, had barged into the secretaries' room. It may have been by chance though, quite possibly, she had been alerted that something big was going on by her lover's excitement after the earlier calls from de Gaulle.

As Spears handed the sheets of paper to a typist, the short, domineering Countess scanned them over the male secretary's shoulder. 'It was difficult to tell from her expression whether rage or amazement prevailed,' the British general, who loathed her, wrote. 'Both feelings were apparent.'[9]

Spears told the secretary to get on with the job, but the Countess went on delaying him to read Reynaud's scrawl. She was used to exploiting her position. She had been known to take secret documents from the Premier's desk – one was found in her bed. In league with two of the leading pro-armistice politicians in the government, she could now tell them what she had learned by leaning over the secretary's shoulder.

Though London hoped that the union proposal would bolster French morale, it would have no effect on the immediate situation on the battlefield. So the order went out to continue to remove or destroy military equipment to prevent it falling into German hands. Having done all they could, soldiers were then to head for the last escape point at St-Nazaire.

'We wrecked everything we could,' recalled Lance Corporal Fred Coe, who had joined the army as a boy cadet at the age of nine after his mother's death. His Royal Army Service Corps unit put hundreds of vehicles out of commission before moving out of their base near Nantes.

Not everything was destroyed at St-Etienne-de-Montluc as the motor transport detachment shuttled lorryloads of equipment to be taken off from St-Nazaire. A convoy that left at 6 a.m. contained transformers, hand tools and stores. The soldiers also wanted to move heavy equipment down the Loire to the sea, but the French refused to provide tugs to pull the barges.

After the second convoy left, they were told that no more

materiel could be taken – every available vehicle was needed to carry troops. As their unit's report noted: 'Men's lives were considered more valuable than stores.'[10] The crank cases and cylinder blocks of vehicles under repair were smashed. Axles were severed with oxyacetylene cutters. A hole was dug to house equipment which might be used again if they ever returned.

At 7 a.m., the whole unit was summoned to the parade ground. They were told that they would now stage a rapid move to the coast, taking one pack each with them. 'All orders, or counter orders,' the instructions added, 'to be obeyed implicitly, no matter how trivial they might appear at the time'. Civilians must not be told where they were going. They were reminded of Dunkirk and how 'the fighting spirit and the will to win through would probably save an apparently hopeless situation'.

Acid was poured over the Quarter Master's stores. The 'Shunting Engine', a five-ton transportable crane, was destroyed. Everything except for buildings was either removed or made useless. At 10.02 a.m., the Motor Transport unit drove out in trucks. They had no food or water with them; some would not have anything to eat for forty-eight hours.

Another convoy of lorries found itself slowed down by a Frenchman driving a horse-drawn cart on which a canal barge was loaded. The British stopped him, threw the boat into a ditch and chased the horses into a field. When they got to the airfield outside St-Nazaire, they were told that everything they had brought must be dumped and set alight. The order from London was 'save the men and destroy everything'.

The departure for St-Nazaire of the Royal Engineers unit

to which Neville Chesterton returned after hearing rumours of surrender at the cinema was delayed not once but twice.

First, it was the fault of his friend Derek, whom Chesterton described as habitually looking as if he had a hangover. When the men were told to fall in to march off, Derek was missing; he was found shaving, his pack slung on his back the wrong way up. He was ordered into line immediately, half his face still covered with lather. 'If there are more soldiers like you,' the red-faced sergeant major bellowed,' God help us.'

Then the unit's captain could not find his helmet. He refused to leave without it, so a search was mounted. The headgear was discovered, and the fifty-man unit finally left. After a while, it found three abandoned army lorries on the road. The unit's motorcycle riders got into the driving seats, but, unfamiliar with the gears, they moved forward only slowly. The delays and the slow pace of the trucks may well have saved their lives.

In Nantes, the men left at the base ordnance depot, who had been packing stores to be moved to the coast, received fresh instructions – they were to get out and leave the supplies behind. 'Everything was thrown open,' 19-year-old Henry Harding from Wales recalled. 'You could help yourself to whatever it was you wanted, so we took chocolate.'

Joe Sweeney, who had arranged for the reunion in the café at Nantes between his friend, Les, and Thérèse from Belgium, replaced the army gear in his kitbag and backpack with tins of Players No. 3 from the open NAAFI stores. Another group of men took boxes of Woodbine cigarettes and kidney-shaped tins of ham from an abandoned military store. An officer stuck a bottle of Johnny Walker and a bottle of Vichy water in a pair of rubber boots strung round his neck on a piece of string.

When the French Cabinet met in Bordeaux on the evening of 16 June, Reynaud read the British document on Franco-British union twice. His optimism swiftly crumbled as he came under violent attack. Marshal Pétain called the idea 'fusion with a corpse'. Others saw it as a British attempt to exercise dominion over France, or to grab the French Empire.

Pressure for peace had been raised by the neatly timed reading of a cable from the front announcing another defeat, and calling for an immediate decision on a truce. Tempers flared as the tough Interior Minister, Georges Mandel, called a leading pro-armistice minister a coward. But opposition to the union was such that no vote was taken on the proposal from London.

At 7.30 p.m., Reynaud called in General Spears and the ambassador, Ronald Campbell. The Premier appeared relieved. It was, Spears wrote, 'as if, walking into a room to console a widower, one was confronted by a bridegroom'. After the British visitors left, Reynaud went to the drawing room to join the Comtesse de Portes, and read to her a telegram he was about to send to Roosevelt saying he was stepping down. At 8 p.m., he formally submitted his resignation to President Lebrun.

As they left the Premier's office, Campbell and Spears found de Gaulle waiting between the dark columns of the entrance hall, his face pale. He said Weygand was going to have him arrested. He wanted to go to London.

After consulting Churchill, Spears arranged to fly the French general out aboard his plane the following morning.

De Gaulle then went to see Reynaud to say he was leaving for Britain. The Premier handed him 100,000 francs from secret government funds.

At the Bordeaux préfecture, the Interior Minister, Mandel, sat at a desk at the end of a long gallery lit by candles. Spears went to urge him to join de Gaulle on the flight to London the following day.

'You fear for me because I am a Jew,' Mandel replied. 'Well, it is just because I am a Jew that I will not go tomorrow; it would look as though I was afraid, as if I was running away. Wednesday, perhaps.'

'It may be too late,' Spears argued.

'I will not go tomorrow,' the Frenchman insisted.

Just then, Mandel's mistress popped her head round the door, and said their bags were packed. They were leaving Bordeaux, but not France.

'*À bientôt, à très bientôt à Londres, j'espère,*' – 'See you soon, very soon, in London, I hope' – Spears said as he left.[11]

Unaware of what had happened in Bordeaux, Churchill ate dinner before being driven to Waterloo station to take the train to Southampton, where he would board a cruiser to meet Reynaud in Concarneau. As he prepared to leave Downing Street, a terse telegram arrived from the ambassador, Campbell: 'Meeting cancelled, message follows.'

Unready to accept the news, Churchill still got into his car for the station. His wife went to see him off. At Waterloo, the Prime Minister boarded the train, and sat in his compartment while the locomotive got up steam. Hastings 'Pug' Ismay, Churchill's military aide, and the naval commander, Admiral Dudley Pound, urged him to give up the trip, but Churchill sat where he was for half an hour, as if the sheer exercise of his will power could prevent the ally across the Channel from falling apart. Then reality took hold, and he returned to Downing Street where a further message from Campbell gave details of the crisis which had erupted in Bordeaux.

At 11.30 p.m., French radio announced that Philippe Pétain had been asked to form a new administration; the new Premier said he was making 'the gift of myself to France to lessen her misfortune'. Weygand would take second rank in the government. Peace advocates got other senior posts.

At 1 a.m., the Foreign Minister, Paul Baudouin, told Campbell that France was going to ask Germany for its armistice terms. An hour later, Churchill telephoned Pétain. He warned the French leaders that giving up the fight would 'scarify their names for a thousand years of history'.[12] One senior British civil servant called the Prime Minister's message 'scorching'. Another described it as 'the most violent conversation I ever heard Churchill conduct. He only spoke so roughly because he felt that anger might sway the old Marshal when nothing else would.'

But Pétain was past swaying. Campbell reported that he and Weygand were 'living in another world, and imagined that they could sit round a green table discussing armistice terms in the old manner'. The Marshal's grasp of affairs was tenuous. He fell asleep during meetings, and was said to enjoy 'an hour of lucidity a day'. But there was one thing he firmly believed in – the need to end the war as soon as possible. A tongue lashing from London was not going to make any difference, even at 2 a.m. Though some army units would put up resistance, the Battle of France was over and the task of rescuing troops remaining across the Channel became even more urgent.

*

Between 16,000 and 17,000 troops were taken off from St-Nazaire by midnight on 16 June, most on the big British and Polish boats lying in Quiberon Bay. Among them were a handful of officers who had abandoned their men to get to the troopship, the *Georgic*. Though it was not known exactly how many men were still waiting to be embarked, and some had left directly from Nantes, the number was rising as more troops came into the town. The combined total of soldiers and airmen who passed through St-Nazaire was equal to its population of 47,000.

Still, the war diary of the British command in Nantes shows no great urgency in the orders for evacuation.[13] Though the Luftwaffe was stepping up air raids on western France, German tanks and troops were some way up the Loire, moving towards Angers. Messages concerning the rescue ships envisaged a five-day operation. One problem was settled when it was decided to hand over 400 mules of the Indian Transport Company to the French, rather than trying to embark them for England.

The British forces in and around St-Nazaire were made up of a huge patchwork of units. There were men from the Royal Artillery, the Sherwood Foresters, the Royal Welch Fusiliers, the Argyll & Sutherland Highlanders, the Buffs of the Royal East Kent Regiment, the King's Own Yorkshire Light Infantry, the Essex, East Surrey and Cheshire regiments. There were units of the Royal Engineers, the Royal Ordnance Corps, the Auxiliary Military Pioneer Corps and the Pay Corps, along with RAF ground crew and support forces, soldiers who had manned bases in Dieppe and Nantes, members of the Church Army, the Salvation Army and the YMCA. There were also the civilians from the Fairey aircraft factory in Belgium who had travelled up the west coast by train.

A report by the British garrison in the port recorded that, given prevailing conditions, the hours of waiting, the lack of food or water and the air-raid alarms, 'the conduct of the men was very satisfactory'.[14] But one officer noted that some of the troops took the law into their own hands, and some officers argued among themselves about whose units should go first.

The harbour was covered with a pall of smoke from the repeated bombing raids, one of which sank a French minesweeper. There was a lot of gunfire when the German planes attacked. Wing Commander Macfadyen watched 'an amazing display of pyrotechnics' as French troops fired at aircraft far out of range of their light guns. Spent bullets fell on the men on the docks – one hit the Wing Commander's steel helmet.

On one side of the main embarkation quay, piles of army coats were stuck up on sticks to look like soldiers standing in a single file. The deception attracted some of the strafing aircraft, but the real troops still had to dodge the ricocheting bullets as they passed along the other side to reach the waiting tenders. When an NCO got a piece of shrapnel in his eye, his fellow soldiers bathed the wound and covered it with lint. One man decided to get out – when a call was made for a driver to take a lorry back to Nantes to collect troops there, he stepped forward, and probably saved his life.

At 10 p.m. on 16 June, the French admiral in charge of the port of St-Nazaire ordered the embarkation to be stopped for the night. He feared that lights would be used in the evacuation, and that this would allow the planes to see targets more clearly – in fact, given the full moon and calm sea, no illumination would have been needed.

Some troops tried to sleep in the street or on the cobbles of the town's main square. Others went to a cobblestoned jetty with a small lighthouse or wandered along the quay by the estuary looking out across the water to the flat coastline on the other side of the Loire. On the beach, a group of men found a cache of West Indian rum, and got drunk, waking late the next morning. A unit from the RAS Corps crawled into some empty barrels to sleep.

Men congregated in bars, singing and shouting as they drank. Officers organised meals of bully beef and biscuits. Strong tea was a constant source of comfort. One man got his comrades to smash up wooden boxes to light a fire, and brewed tea in old petrol cans – soon he had a long queue waiting for char.

Lying in a gutter, Sidney Dunmall of the Pay Corps, who had dived for cover twice when the German plane flew over his unit marching towards the coast, tried to sleep, using his respirator as a pillow. Getting hungry, he went to the sea wall to join some comrades who had two tins of bully beef. But somebody knocked them into the sea by mistake, so they had to make do with bread. After that, their sergeant major told them to get into slit trenches on the seafront because an air raid was coming. 'All Hell broke loose as the ack ack battery behind us blazed away like mad,' Dunmall recalled. When the planes left, he finally got to sleep.

The civilians from the Fairey aircraft works in Belgium, who had travelled down to Bordeaux and then up the west coast, arrived in St-Nazaire on 16 June. Roger Legroux, the

11-year-old son of a Fairey manager, saw the sea shore covered with troops and materiel. More vehicles and men were arriving. The planes went on bombing into the night as the Legroux family slept in a lorry; some of the other civilians passed the night in cars. The civilians discussed what to do next. Afraid of being sunk on the way across to Britain, some decided to return to Belgium. Roger's father said that, having come so far, they should go on.

Leonard Forde, the radio operator from the Royal Corps of Signals who had driven his 'gin palace' wireless truck across France, abandoned it after arriving at St-Nazaire. He shot holes in the radio set, and ran down to the beach to join a crowd there. Ravenously hungry, he also longed for a smoke.

On the beach, there was a huge pile of NAAFI supplies, including cigarettes. Forde and several other men tried to get at them, but military policemen waved them away. When the soldiers insisted, the police drew revolvers, so they retreated.

Soon afterwards, German dive bombers swooped, apparently mistaking the pile of supplies for a petrol or military dump. Forde and his companions threw themselves on the ground. There was a tremendous explosion, and thousands of cigarettes were blown sky-high. Some of the men managed to grab a handful.

'A very good feeling was evident in the local inhabitants,' the British garrison report noted of the people of St-Nazaire.[15] Women plied Joe Sweeney's unit with sandwiches and wine as they marched into the town; children were sent after the men to collect the empty glasses.

Still, there were some signs of hostility. Pipe-smoking Donald Draycott, who had worked in a ground crew for Fairey bombers before joining the move west, heard windows opening, and French people shouting curses at the British because they were leaving. Some locals threw things at the troops. Draycott could not see what they were in the dark, but thought they sounded like household utensils. On the quay, a French soldier spat at the feet of a British officer who had bade him farewell.

To begin with, local inhabitants thought the British had come to help defend the town, but soon realised that they were heading home. On his way to the docks, a French-speaking sergeant saw an old woman looking from a window.

'*Ah, vous anglais vous allez partir?*' – 'Ah, are you English leaving?' – she said.

'*Oui, Madame, [mais] nous reviendrons,*' – 'Yes, Madame, [but] we will return' – he replied.

'*Non, non, tout est fini!*' – 'No, no, it's all over.' – she said emphatically.

Sergeant Macpherson of the RAF recalled hearing local people saying '*Pauvres enfants*' – 'Poor young things' – as they passed.

On the outskirts of St-Nazaire, a shopkeeper refused to sell food to Wilfred Oldham of the Royal Signals until the soldier pointed his rifle at him. Later, wandering on the beach at nightfall, Oldham met a Belgian girl who told him of a house where he could sleep on the floor. He found twenty-eight women there, all refugees. In the morning, he went back to the beach. There, he heard a voice calling 'Vilfred.' It was the Belgian girl. She handed him a slice of bread spread with marmalade.

CHAPTER 4

———

Monday, 17 June 1940

THE *LANCASTRIA* ENTERED the wide estuary of the Loire off St-Nazaire in the early hours of 17 June to join the evacuation of Operation Aerial. Frank Brogden, an electrician from Bolton who had signed up for the Merchant Navy at the age of thirteen and had looked after the loudspeakers and the sound equipment for the ship's cinema in peacetime, was on the midnight to 4 a.m. watch. He remembered the sea as being very calm under a full moon.

'You would never think there was any war on,' he recalled. 'We might have been going down on a cruise. It seemed very pleasant.' But then, when the ship sailed on in the cool, bright dawn, he saw smoke from fires on the shore. Standing on the bridge in the dawning light, Harry Grattidge could hear the throbbing of planes not far away.

As well as the *Lancastria*, thirty or so evacuation boats had gathered in the bay. Among them were two destroyers, the *Havelock* and the *Highlander*, which had taken part in the evacuation from Norway earlier in the month, and the *Cambridgeshire*, an armoured trawler from Grimsby with a single 1.47 gun. The convoy of six ships that had come down the Bristol Channel included a smart new freighter, the *John Holt*. There was also a converted pleasure boat previously used by the Wills tobacco company, with marketing slogans still written on the walls of her main cabin.

The estuary outside St-Nazaire is broad but shallow, and subject to strong tides. Only the smaller boats of the flotilla could get into the harbour; and even they had only a window of three hours on each side of high tide in which to pick up men.

Captain Sharp anchored the *Lancastria* four miles out in the Charpentier Roads, opposite the Pointe de St-Gildas where legend had it that an ancient holy man had left the imprint of his foot and staff in the rocks. A British hospital ship lay nearby, filled with patients and medical personnel. The sea at that point was twelve fathoms deep.

At around 5 a.m., a British naval transport officer came out to make arrangements with Sharp. The Captain said the *Lancastria* could accommodate 3000 people.

'You will have to try and take as many as possible,' he was told.[1]

'Is this another capitulation,' Grattidge asked, remembering Norway.

The officer looked shocked.

'Don't even mention the word,' he said. 'It's merely a temporary movement of troops.'

If the officer deceived himself, Grattidge wrote later, he deceived nobody else.

On shore, the French harbour authorities delayed the start of the embarkation by refusing to open the gates of a lock. British naval officers concluded that 'the worm of defeat was already evident'. After much argument, the gates were opened and troops were taken out into the bay on destroyers, tugs, fishing boats and other small craft. When Frank Brogden finished his watch and went down to his berth at 6.30 a.m., men were starting to arrive.

It was no simple matter to manoeuvre from the harbour. The boats had to leave stern first, turn round a buoy and then point themselves out into the estuary. This was made more complicated by the cross tide and the presence of so many small craft.

The captain of HMS *Havelock*, Barry Stevens, who was in charge of the naval flotilla, was so tired that he handed over command to a first lieutenant who misjudged the turn out of the dock, and wrapped the buoy's mooring cable round the destroyer's starboard propeller shaft. With 500 men on board, the *Havelock* was a sitting target for German bombers.

The first French tug it hailed to give assistance sailed on by. A second dragged her out into the estuary, the buoy and its cable putting one propeller out of action. Captain Stevens transferred to another destroyer, the *Highlander*, which was also taking men out to the *Lancastria*.

As it came alongside, Harry Grattidge recognised the *Highlander* from the Norwegian evacuation. An officer on the destroyer shouted across to ask for a hawser with which to tie up to the troopship. Grattidge said he could supply one, but would want a receipt. The officer gave a cynical laugh. 'You can have the receipt,' he said. 'You'll be lucky if you get home.'

Denise Petit from the Banque de France recognised a British captain she had got to know lining up his men outside the Port Office. The distress on his face brought tears to her eyes. Despite his own sadness, he tried to comfort her. But neither of them could find the right words, and he went off. 'Will I ever hear from him?' she asked in her diary.

Vic Flowers, the RAF wireless operator who had seen 'Cobber' Kain crash to his death and had then avoided being dragooned into flying himself, arrived in St-Nazaire with a group of other ground crewmen and some officers very early in the morning of 17 June. They marched through streets strewn with masses of discarded uniforms, webbing and kitbags. Here and there, rifles had been left propped against walls.

They crossed a narrow bridge to the main embarkation point, a 380-yard long dock called the Forme Joubert where the great transatlantic liner, the *Normandie*, had been built. A fleet of small boats was waiting. Flowers thought at first that they were going to take them all the way back to England, and was surprised at how small they were. Men crowded together on board like sheep called out 'Baa, Baa.' They explained to Flowers and his comrades that the boat was just going to ferry them to a big ship waiting in the estuary, the *Lancastria*.

*

At the airfield outside St-Nazaire, several units were ordered to move off between 2.30 and 3 a.m. – marching under cover of night to avoid the attention of German aircraft. The transport workers from St-Etienne-de-Montluc sheltered under hayricks when the Luftwaffe flew overhead. Some First World War veterans on the road shot their rifles up in the air. Fred Coe's company of the Royal Army Service Corps fired at one plane, but missed. During the three-hour march to the docks, Coe recalled, the men were in good spirits: they were going home at last.

The men from St-Etienne-de-Montluc found their journey slowed down by an RAF contingent which had left just before them. The airmen were carrying so many suitcases and bags that 'they could hardly crawl,' the unit's report recorded.[3] They stopped to rest every half-mile, but would not let the mechanics go ahead of them.

Reaching the docks, the Motor Transport commander stationed a guard to make sure that no other units jumped the queue. His men still had to wait for ninety minutes while the RAF group embarked on a tug, their cases hampering their progress as they negotiated a difficult gangway. In contrast, the army report noted with satisfaction, the Motor Transport men made it on to their boat in half an hour. But, arriving at the *Lancastria*, they had to wait again while the RAF 'struggled on board'.

Other army units resented the way the airmen had moved ahead of them down the middle of the quay while the soldiers were kept to the sides. Tom Beattie of the RAF heard a trooper saying, 'The Brylcreem boys are going on first.' For everybody, the imperative was to board a boat for the big liner lying out in the bay.

Arriving at 4.30 a.m., Wing Commander Macfadyen

ordered his men to spread out on the docks to prevent other units jumping the queue. A German air attack could have mown down the crowd of stationary men.

Edwin Quittenton of the Royal Engineers spent eighteen hours hiding in fields from strafing attacks or sleeping in a car with two majors and a captain. At 3.30 a.m. on 17 June, the four men were woken by a shout – it was time to get ready to move down to the port. Half an hour later, they set off, on foot. Quittenton rejoiced. 'We were going home!'

On one of the piers, four chaplains sat on a stack of luggage. They wore khaki uniforms with clerical collars. They were weeping.

The destroyer, HMS *Havelock*, pulled into the quay, and lowered a gangplank. 'Are you buggers coming?' a marine shouted to the chaplains. 'We can't come back again and we can't take any bloody luggage.' When the churchmen did not move, the boat pulled 100 yards away from the dockside.

Further along the pier, Joe Sweeney and another man found four bottles of rum abandoned on steps leading down to the sea. The two of them emptied their water bottles and filled them – and their mugs – with the alcohol. Then they walked back.

Sweeney, the fair-haired Scot from Newcastle who had driven a Humber Snipe staff car to St-Nazaire, offered a mug of rum to one of the weeping chaplains. The clergyman sipped at the liquor, and nearly choked. He held out his mug to another of the chaplains, who also had trouble getting the drink down. But the other two clergymen emptied the mugs they were offered in one gulp without saying anything, and stopped weeping.

Despite what the marine had said, the *Havelock* did come back. It lowered its gangplank again, and the marine screamed at the chaplains to come on board to be taken to the *Lancastria*. This time they did so, leaving their luggage behind. One called out to Sweeney and the men round him: 'Take what you like from the luggage, but when you get back to England give the stuff to the first church you see: it doesn't matter whether it is Roman Catholic or Church of England.'

There was an immediate rush to get at the luggage. Sweeney opened a briefcase. Inside was a portable altar. The men snatched at its pieces; Sweeney slipped a miniature diamond-studded chalice into a trouser pocket – to make room for it, he threw away a tin of cigarettes. He intended to hand it in to the first church he came across once he was back in England.

Orders were issued that men could board with only one kitbag or case, plus what they could carry by hand. A sergeant in the Pay Corps sat on the quay emptying two haversacks stuffed with clocks, watches and other souvenirs he had collected. Sergeant Macpherson of the RAF had 'a rare old sort out and regretfully jettisoned some nice and risqué Parisian magazines'.

Some got round the instruction, or interpreted it liberally. Sergeant George Youngs held on to his chromium-plated French bicycle, with dynamo lighting and a musical horn; there were complaints about the space it took up, but nobody made him abandon it. An army padre took a pale blue Lilo with him. Despite quarantine regulations, two or three men carried dogs, and one an angora rabbit.

Following the orders to destroy what could not be removed, an RAF driver set the motor of his Dodge lorry going, jumped out and watched it tip over the quay into the sea. Dispatch riders did the same with their motorcycles.

But Captain Griggs, who had sampled the wares of bistros while driving to St-Nazaire, got four suitcases out of his blue Vauxhall saloon, and persuaded a quartet of sappers to carry one each on board. Then he located some petrol, had the car's tank filled and handed the keys to his French interpreter.

Somewhere in the sky above, a small plane was flying alone up the west coast of France. On board were the British general, Edward Spears, and Charles de Gaulle, who looked fixedly ahead. Soon after leaving Bordeaux, they had passed over a French passenger ship, the *Champlain*, which had been sunk by the Germans and was lying on her side, surrounded by hundreds of men in the water. Whether they looked down at the evacuation armada assembled in the Loire estuary is not recorded, but, over Brittany, Spears saw great palls of smoke rising from burning fuel dumps.

Landing in Jersey, the British general asked de Gaulle if he wanted something to drink. The Frenchman asked for coffee. When it came, he sipped it and said, 'Very good tea.' No, Spears told him, this was English coffee.

As they flew on to London, Marshal Pétain went on the radio to tell the nation that, thirty-eight days after the German attack, hostilities must cease and France must open negotiations for an armistice. (When the speech was rebroadcast later in the day, that passage was changed to 'We must try to cease hostilities', but the semantics meant nothing.)

'It is with a heavy heart that I say we must cease to fight,' the Marshal went on in his high, reedy voice. 'I have applied to our opponent to ask him if he is ready to sign with us, as between soldiers after the fight and in honour, a means to put an end to hostilities. Let all Frenchmen group themselves around the government over which I preside during this painful trial and affirm once more their faith in the destiny of our country.' As the Marshal spoke, Rommel's Panzers were advancing 150 miles in a single day to reach the port of Cherbourg, while other German units were pressing towards the estuary of the Loire.

At his 'Wolf's Gorge' headquarters in Belgium, Hitler threw out his arms, laughed and slapped his thigh in delight when told that France was seeking an armistice, jerking up one knee in an involuntary jump for joy. With one of his two main adversaries dropping out of the conflict, and his eastern front secured by the non-aggression pact reached with the Soviet Union the previous year, it seemed only a matter of time before Britain, too, would fall.

Across the Channel, the War Cabinet assembled in London at 11 a.m. One topic for discussions was whether the BEF commander, Alan Brooke, should remain in France. Churchill said he hoped the General would stay so long as his presence could be of value to 'the difficult withdrawal' the British troops faced.

Brooke was at his headquarters in the town of Redon, north of St-Nazaire, when he learned of the French decision to seek an armistice. A French liaison officer came to see him with the news, collapsing in tears as he did so.

'This renders the situation very critical lest negotiations should lead to the internment of British troops in France!' the trim, moustachioed British Commander noted in his diary. 'It is essential for us to get away early.'[4] His mission was ending as badly as he had foreseen.

He telephoned London, trying to speak to the Chief of the Imperial General Staff. But Sir John Dill was not available. When Brooke tried again forty-five minutes later, he was told that communications with London had been cut.

So he got into his car and was driven towards St-Nazaire to go home with the last of his troops. In a letter to his wife, he noted that he was 'feeling wonderfully fit'.

The small boats ferrying men out to the *Lancastria* took three to four hours for the round trip. Most carried 500 or so men. They were often machine-gunned by German planes, but none appears to have been hit. Mines dropped by the Luftwaffe were another hazard though, again, none of the tenders was damaged.

On the way out, there were some private moments. Joe Saxton of the Sherwood Forester did not have a wallet, and had given a photograph of his girlfriend, Lily, to another soldier, who did, for safe keeping. Now, in one of the tenders going to the *Lancastria*, he asked to have a look. Gazing at the picture, he said: 'Well, sweetheart it won't be long now, we shall soon be together.' Then he handed it back.

After the weeks of uncertainty and retreat across France, the *Lancastria* offered the prospect of security, and a safe way home. Tired as the men coming on board were, the ship's electrician, Frank Brogden, detected a special look in their eyes. 'We've made it,' it said. 'We're going home.' They felt as if they were back in Britain. Some kissed the deck. A civilian woman told one of the ship's waiters, Joe O'Brien, that she 'felt so safe on an English ship'.

Many of them had never been outside Britain before being posted to France, or been on a ship, let alone one like the *Lancastria*. They were awed by her size. 'It was the first big ship I had been on in my life,' Fred Coe remarked. 'I'd never seen so many people.'

An RAF man, Peter Walker Vinicombe, who had spent the night with his unit sitting in the street, recalled it as 'a great hulk . . . a gigantic ship as far as we were concerned'. When his tender came alongside and he joined others climbing up nets hung down the hull, the liner's sides seemed to just go straight up into the sky.

Seeing how enormous the *Lancastria* was, Stan Flowers concluded that she had been sent to take them on a long voyage, maybe to the Far East. Another soldier thought she looked 'as solid as the Strand Palace Hotel'.

Early arrivals stepping through the doors on the ship's side were met by two stewards in white uniforms with gold buttons. One steward noted down each man's name, regiment and unit, while the other handed out small cards marked with the number of a cabin or berth, and a ticket for the dining room. They asked the men not to damage the walls or the furniture. As they moved into the ship, some of the troops picked up life jackets from a pile on the deck, thinking they would come in useful as pillows during the voyage.

While the soldiers and RAF men were anxious to get on board and find a place to rest, there was no sense of urgency.

A chaplain who had been taken down to the docks in his car by a driver noted that those going aboard were doing so in what appeared to be 'a very leisurely manner'. No one seemed to think there was any hurry. As he stood on the deck watching the troops, the chaplain remarked to a man beside him: 'It looks as though we have all day.'

As the thirty civilians from the Fairey aircraft factory came on board, soldiers handed the children English coins. The men were allocated a cabin to share between them; wives and children were given one for each family.

Roger Legroux felt very excited – 'eleven years old, getting on a big ship and going across the ocean to another country'. When his parents took him to the dining room, he was overcome by its opulence, and had his first taste of a yellow, round fruit he had never seen before – a grapefruit.

For some, the first priority was to find a bathroom for a wash and shave. Others headed for the barber's shop. Men feeling ill checked in to the sickbay.

Two friends, Sid Keenan and John Broadbent, struggled through the crush of men, and went below in search of a bathroom. At the foot of a staircase, they spotted a door marked 'Officers Only'. Disregarding the instruction, they looked inside and saw a large bath. They went in, and bolted the door. John ran a bath, took off his clothes and got into the water, while Sid shaved.

Sapper Norman Driver, of the Royal Engineers, located a cabin with two toilets and a wash bowl. With him were three friends – Cal Beal from Sheffield, Burt Cunliffe from Warrington, and George Watling from London who always carried a piece of his girlfriend's dress with him. As he washed

The *Lancastria* leaves Liverpool in her Cunard colours in her pre-war glory days. She was, a crew member recalled, a 'very, very happy ship'.

The ornate salon where passengers dined in peacetime and hundreds of men would be trapped in June 1940.

Captain Rudolph Sharp, a man with a horror of war.

Chief Officer Harry Grattidge, future 'Captain of the Queens', who would walk out onto the sea.

Troops lining up on the docks at St-Nazaire to be evacuated. The *Lancastria* was their goal.

Heading for home.

The *Highlander* jammed with men being taken out to the *Lancastria.*

The JU-88, pride of the Luftwaffe and nemesis of the *Lancastria.*

The liner starts to go down after the bombing.

The *Lancastria*'s last moments as men crowd on the upturned hull and plunge into the sea.

Survivors, some naked, most covered in oil, cram on to a rescue vessel.

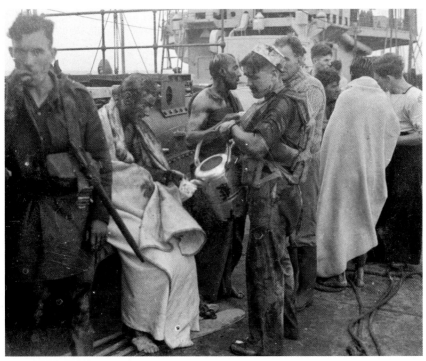

Tea – hot and sweet – was a great comfort.

Sister Chamley of the Church Army, who handed her life belt to a soldier.

Stan Flowers got a will to live when he remembered it was his mother's birthday.

Wally Smith shook hands with his friend Stan Flowers before jumping from the liner. He was never seen alive again.

Fred Coe, former boy soldier and Bren gunner on the *Lancastria* who was pulled from the water on to a rescue boat.

General Alan Brooke (centre), who had masterminded the second evacuation from France, with survivors and his staff on the voyage home.

British newspapers reported the disaster – six weeks later and for one day.

LANCASTRIA SANK WITH 5,300 ABOARD

2,477 SAVED: SURVIVORS TELL OF NAZI MACHINE-GUNNING

Details were released last night of the sinking by enemy action on June 17 of the 16,243-ton Cunard-White Star liner Lancastria off St. Nazaire.

The Lancastria was being used as a transport in the evacuation of British troops and civilian refugees from France. Nearly 2,500 are known to have been saved from a total of about 5,350 on board. It is thought, however, that others may have made their way ashore and fallen into enemy hands.

The first news of the loss of the Lancastria, given in the later editions of THE DAILY TELEGRAPH yes-

was too small to float, but none of them would let go.

"As our boat moved away from the side of the ship, soldiers watching through a porthole saw that we were wearing our lifebelts. They shouted, 'Give us a chance,' and we took off the belts and flung them into the sea. The soldiers jumped in after them."

A cook told how he saw one soldier grab a young girl, both of whose legs had been broken. He swam with her and both were picked up, but she died later on the rescuing ship and was buried on the voyage over

COVERED WITH OIL

Most of the men who survived were swimming in the oily water for an hour or more before they were

Churchill thought the press had had quite enough bad news. So he ordered that the disaster was not to be covered.

Jacqueline Tillyard, who floated away from the ship in her mother's arms at the age of two.

Jacqueline Tillyard with Joan Rodes (right), the 'Angel of St-Nazaire' who crossed the bay on a rescue boat though pregnant.

Joan Rodes with two men she helped to save, Percy Fairfax (left) and George Youngs (right).

Survivors at the memorial service in London in 2004. Fred Coe holds the standard of the Lancastria Association; at the other end of the seat is Denis Maloney whose boat rescued Coe on 17 June 1940.

and shaved, Driver thought that he was getting 'ready for Blighty'.

Sergeant George Youngs left his gleaming bicycle in a safe place on the deck to go for a shave. Padre Captain Charles McMenemy took time to do the same, and then lay down on the floor of his cabin on his pale blue Lilo to get some sleep. Major Scott-Bowden, the officer who carried bottles of Johnny Walker and Vichy water in a pair of rubber boots strung round his neck, found seven officers already in the four-bunk cabin he had been allocated. He went to see the ship's purser, who told him, 'Sorry, Sir, but that's the best I can do.' So he had a warm bath of sea water, and, returning to his cabin, made room on a bunk to have a rest.

An army baker, G. F. Crew, who had not washed for a week, sought out a bathroom, but four or five men were already there, in the tub or sitting on its sides. The newcomer took off his uniform and climbed in. Though he rubbed soap all over his body, he could get no lather from the water which was drawn from the sea. The other men laughed, and told him he was 'a silly sod'.

After a shower, Joe Sweeney donned a clean shirt and underwear. He put the jewelled chalice from the chaplain's briefcase into one of his boots, and then stuffed both of them with tins of fifty Players No.3 cigarettes he had removed from a NAAFI store. Having hidden his boots behind a ventilator vent, he went to the dining room for breakfast of sausages, bacon and eggs, and hot buttered toast. Feeling like a new man, he returned to his cabin and dropped off to sleep.

Soon, the crush of men brought out from St-Nazaire was such that it became impossible to register each one individually.

The cabins filled far beyond their usual capacity; men were left to find any place they could.

With German planes flying overhead, some officers considered it safest to move their units to shelter down below. One group of 800 RAF men was told to head for a dimly lit hold where mattresses and palliasses were laid on the floor. Donald Draycott, from a ground crew that had been based in Nantes, thought the hold resembled a morgue. If the *Lancastria* was attacked by submarines or hit a mine on the way home, there would be no chance of getting out. The liner, he noticed, did not have proper working gangways like a purpose-built troopship. So he decided to go up on deck.

A ginger-haired soldier, Stanley Rimmer, also had his doubts. He remembered advice he had been given by his brother, who was in the navy: 'If you are ever on a troopship, try to avoid going down into the hold.' So, though he followed orders from his sergeant to go below, he later climbed to an upper deck.

Stan Flowers and 400 men from the transport repair unit at St-Etienne-de-Montluc were sent to a big hold where they sat and waited for the liner to move, some passing the time by playing cards. A detachment of Royal Engineers was directed to the bottom of the ship, aft of the engine room. It was stuffy and warm down there, and they were soon nodding off. After a couple of hours, they woke one another up to eat tinned rations. Then they settled down for another sleep. An air raid had been reported, but that did not bother anyone.

One man decided at the last moment that he did not want to go to the *Lancastria*. As he mounted the gangplank to the tender, Vic Flowers was overcome by an urge to turn back.

Though men were moving up behind him, he suddenly knew that nothing was going to make him leave dry land.

Climbing to the outside of the gangplank, Flowers held on to the rail and got back on shore, his progress eased by his lack of kit. Two other RAF men followed him.

A military policeman shouted at them to get back on to the tender, but they ran off through the crowd on the docks. Walking to cliffs overlooking the harbour, they introduced themselves to one another.

When the *Lancastria*'s electrician, Frank Brogden, went back on duty after sleeping for five hours following his early morning watch, he was amazed at the number of men who had boarded the liner. He had never seen so many troops in his life. They seemed to be everywhere. If there was a two-foot space on the decks, it would immediately be filled.

Like Joe Sweeney, the lucky ones enjoyed a hearty breakfast – bacon, egg and sausages in onion gravy, porridge, grapefruit, toast and marmalade, washed down with tea and coffee.

But some complained that they could not get anything to eat. One man was so hungry that he ate a piece of bread covered with oil and grease which he saw on the deck. Exploring the ship after taking a bath, another found a food store with sides of meat hanging from hooks. He asked a sailor for a piece to chew, but was told it was being kept for a long voyage the liner would be making after it dropped off the evacuees.

Others made do with beer. Joe Saxton and a friend got two bottles each, and went to the upper deck to drink them.

When they had finished, they threw them over the side. 'That's a long way to drop,' Saxton's friend said as they watched the bottle falling to the sea.

Captain Clement Stott of the Pay Corps was among those who did get breakfast. As he ate in the 'crowded but beautifully clean and luxurious ship's dining salon', he experienced a feeling of exultation at having brought his fifty men out to safety. An RAF officer with a big moustache talked non-stop at his table. Stott did not take in a word until he heard the other man say he was going to get a drink, and ask if Stott wanted to go with him. 'You bet!' the accountant replied.

A solid mass of people blocked the path to the bar. The main lounge was so full that the steward could hardly make his way through to serve. With everybody shouting for drinks, he told them to form an orderly queue. Stott and his companion got several glasses. 'It was somehow like a picnic and an air of intense excitement hung over the crowd,' he recalled. 'I recognised and chatted with many men I hadn't seen for months and all were inquiring about absent friends. "Where's old so and so?" "Don't know, he buggered off after Dunkirk." "And so and so?" "Poor old boy, bought it near Saint-Valéry."'

At noon, the lunch service began on tables covered with crisp white tablecloths and gleaming cutlery.

The Fairey manager, Legroux, went from the cabin he was sharing with other men to get his wife and two children in their separate quarters so that they could eat together. Fernande Tips, daughter of the managing director of the Fairey branch in Belgium, sat with her mother, two brothers and a maid, all wearing life belts as they ate. A civilian couple, Clifford and Vera Tillyer, were struck by the calm courtesy and efficiency of the white-jacketed stewards who served them as though they were oblivious of the air attacks, the firing and the sirens. Sailors came up to their table and adjusted the tapes of the life belt on their 2-year-old daughter, Jacqueline, so that they would not slip down over her shoulders.

Clement Stott and the men with whom he had been drinking found a table, and settled down for their second meal on the *Lancastria*. 'We ate in such luxury as I hadn't known since the French hotels during the early weeks of the war,' the Pay Corps captain recalled.

The menu listed hors d'oeuvre variés, consommé Massena or thick oxtail soup, followed by fried fillet of cod Colbert, crab salad, macaroni au gratin, sauté of oxtail Nohant, minute steak maître d'hôtel, and boiled knuckle of veal with bacon and parsley sauce. The vegetable selection was green lima beans, and baked, jacket or mashed potatoes. The cold buffet had brawn luncheon sausage, ox tongue, beef and lamb with lettuce, tomatoes and beetroot, and there were cheese and biscuits, rusk pudding, apricot flan and ice cream and wafers to round off the meal. How much of this was actually available is open to question. Soldiers spoke of being served stewed beef and cabbage rather than the delicacies on the menu. Some ate soup from tins.

Still, for men who had trudged through France for weeks, the food was like manna. Sergeant Robert Hill of the Royal Engineers recalled tucking in to a lunch of bangers and mash and tea, while the epicurean Captain Griggs enjoyed 'very good cold meat and salad' at a table he shared with civilians and Salvation Army people.

Coffee came, and the men lit up their cigarettes and pipes. There was a final call for drinks. Nobody at Griggs' table, or anyone else as far as he could tell, was truly aware of how grave the war situation was. 'England has been in a hole before and we always come through,' the Captain reflected. 'So why not again?'

As Captains Stott and Griggs, Sergeant Hill and others on the *Lancastria* enjoyed their lunch, news that France was seeking an armistice reached members of the Luftwaffe's Diving Eagle squadron at their base near Louvain. Peter Stahl and the other German airmen decided that this called for a celebration, continuing the drinking with which they had marked their bombing of the bridge over the Loire at Tours the previous day.

They had hardly begun when they received instructions for a new raid. In flying suits, fur-lined boots, goggles, gloves and sunglasses, they climbed into their fourteen JU-88s to head west, covering in an hour the distance which the British soldiers and ground crews had taken days or weeks to traverse.

This was their longest flight since joining in the Nazi offensive in May. To conserve fuel for the return, Stahl eased up the engine of his aircraft, and dropped behind the other planes. The approach seemed endlessly long to the former test pilot as the squadron crossed First World War battlefields and then flew over lower Normandy and southern Brittany towards France's Atlantic coast. Once again, Stahl was struck by the exodus of civilians and troops on the roads below. All he and his colleagues knew about their target was that it was 'a large concentration of ships in the Loire estuary'.

CHAPTER 5

———

The Bombing

BY THE BEGINNING of the afternoon of 17 June, Harry Grattidge reckoned that 5000 men had come on board. Captain Griggs had taken it upon himself to make a round of the various units to try to find out how many were on the *Lancastria*. He got to 4000, but did not cover anything like the whole boat.

As he stepped on to the ship, one man heard a steward say to another: 'Bloody Hell, that's six thousand and we were supposed to only take four thousand.' Another steward told Morris Wooding, from an RASC Heavy Repair Shops unit: 'God! Six thousand! Never before has the old tub carried so many.' Still more men went on climbing aboard.

A while later, one of the ship's officers was heard to say that the stewards had stopped counting at 6000. A late comer, Samuel Valentine Bardell of the Royal Ordnance Corps, saw a steward with a mechanical clicker: when Bardell asked how many he had counted, the steward replied: 'Oh, we're well over six thousand at the moment.' Another report says a loading officer told a major in the Royal Engineers that he was not going to take any more men as 7000 were already on the liner. Major Fairfax of the RASC recalled hearing one of the ship's officers saying there were 8000 men on the *Lancastria.*

Around lunchtime, Neville Chesterton, the Royal Engineer whose unit had been delayed on its way to St-Nazaire, got into a small French boat with fifty of his comrades to sail into the estuary. German planes swooped to strafe them as they headed out from the shore – to show their esteem for the bravery of the French crew in keeping going, the soldiers handed them all their cigarettes.

As the tender came alongside the *Lancastria,* an officer appeared in the gangway, and shouted, 'You can't come on board. We are full. Go and find another ship.'

'No more, we're overloaded,' a crew member shouted through a loud-hailer at other small boats arriving from St-Nazaire. 'We're not taking any more. We are overcrowded.'

Harry Grattidge ordered the doors on the liner's side to be closed. He refused to take a mooring rope thrown from a destroyer bringing out yet another load of men. In return, there was what the Chief Officer described as 'a volley of mediaeval curses' from the bridge of the other ship.

Turned away, the small boats headed for the other liner moored in the bay, the *Oronsay.* Chesterton felt frustrated that the delay in reaching St-Nazaire had prevented him getting on such an imposing vessel as the *Lancastria.* Leonard Forde, the wireless truck driver, was another disappointed man. Stuck at the back of the crowd on the dockside, he felt his heart sinking as he realised that he would not be able to get on a tender for the *Lancastria*. The men around him groaned at having lost the chance of boarding such a big, fine ship to sail home.

Two of the last who did get on to the liner were a Belgian boy and girl aged about ten, with golden hair and grey eyes. They were on their own except for two dogs, one a pedigree animal, the other a mongrel. Though the children were dirty, they had an air of gravity about them. As they came on to the ship, Harry Grattidge told them that quarantine regulations meant they would have to leave the dogs behind in the tug that had brought them out from St-Nazaire; though a number of soldiers evaded the rules and boarded with their mascot dogs.

Not understanding English, the children looked blankly at him. An elderly woman, described by Grattidge as looking like a vicar's wife, stepped in as interpreter. When she told the children that the dogs would have to be abandoned, the boy's face crumpled. His lips trembled. His grey eyes filled with tears. For a moment, he said nothing, just clinging tightly to the retriever's neck. Then he began to speak, fast and very earnestly, sometimes using the back of his hand to wipe away a tear. Grattidge thought he looked 'very small and defenceless as he stood there and pleaded for his rights like a man'. His sister hugged the mongrel and said nothing.[1]

The woman explained to Grattidge that the children had fled all the way from Belgium on foot, leading their dogs. The Chief Officer found that he could not look the boy in the eye – 'it was like facing up to your own conscience'. So he gave way. Sometimes, the only thing to do with rules was to break them, he reflected. The children boarded with their dogs.

*

Every square foot of space on the decks, in the cabins and down in the holds was filled with dirty, unkempt, exhausted men. Some slept; others played cards. Many did not bother to take life belts that were offered to them – they were tired and thought they had reached safety.

Alec Cuthbert, who had spent the last two days since leaving St-Etienne-de-Montluc without anything to eat, had been among the last to get on board. After enjoying a meal of sausages and mash, he went up on the promenade deck, where he sat with Harry Pack of the Royal Army Service Corps. After a time, Harry decided to go below to fetch some beer but, seeing the crowd at the bar, he gave up and climbed back up to join Alec. Both had life jackets which they used as pillows as they stretched out as best they could on the crowded deck.

Sidney Dunmall, from the Pay Corps, settled down in the sun by the main mast on the fore deck with his kitbag into which he had stuffed 500 cigarettes from the NAAFI stores and a collection of souvenirs from France. He was starving, but, by the time he got down to the dining room, all that was left was boiled cabbage and potatoes. Dunmall said that would be fine, and ate the vegetables with relish. Then he went back to his place on the deck, watching German planes flying overhead with an occasional appearance by British and French fighters.

'Why the hell don't we get cracking and weigh anchor – we're like a sitting duck here,' Teddy Perfect of the Royal Engineers said to his comrades lying with their heads on their kitbags on the upper deck.

The danger became even more apparent when a German plane swooped on the two-funnelled *Oronsay* at 1.48 p.m. One of the bombs it dropped destroyed the liner's bridge, killing several people.

Rudolph Sharp and Harry Grattidge watched the attack from the bridge of the *Lancastria*. Sunlight caught on the wings of the planes with what the Chief Officer described as 'a fine flash of scintillating light, like dragonflies cast in silver'.[2] The two men heard the sharp-edged snarl of the bombs – those that missed the other liner sent up huge spouts of spray that landed on the *Lancastria*'s deck like spring rain. 'At least there's one comfort,' Grattidge said to the Captain. 'We've only got one funnel. They seem to think that because she's got two she's a choicer target.'

The crewman, Michael Sheehan, who had been counting the men coming aboard, went back to his station at the wheel on the bridge, expecting that the liner would be moving off. But Sharp insisted on waiting for an escort. So Sheridan made his way back down the deck, threading a path between the troops lying there, apparently oblivious to the planes attacking the evacuation fleet.

A signal from the commander of the destroyer force, Barry Stevens, was received, saying that, since the *Lancastria* was full, she could leave. Watching the attack on the *Oronsay*, Sharp considered what to do.

Harry Grattidge recalled that the Captain had 'a horror of war and all that it meant'. Also, 'his nerves were more on edge than should happen to any good conscientious seaman who has never thought about death'. There were thousands of men aboard, and the *Lancastria* had only one 4-inch gun as armament, plus a few Bren guns the soldiers had brought with them. She was a sitting duck for the German planes, but leaving the estuary could be equally risky. Sharp had no chart for the area, and there might be German submarines lying in wait out at sea.

Weighing up his options, the Captain sent a message back to the destroyer, asking if he could get protection from a warship. There was no reply.

According to Barry Stevens' papers, the *Lancastria* signalled that she was out of drinking water, and must take on some before sailing.[2] Stevens replied that it would only take eighteen hours to reach Plymouth, so she should leave immediately and not bother about the water. He was unequivocal about where the responsibility for not leaving lay. The *Lancastria*, Stevens wrote, 'had not obeyed the order to sail'.

'I think,' Sharp told Grattidge at last, dragging out his words, 'that we'll do better to wait for the *Oronsay* and go together. What do you think?'

'I think we should stay, sir,' the Chief Officer replied.

So they sent a signal to that effect to the destroyers. As a precaution, Sharp ordered the lifeboats to be swung out in case they were needed. The crew was divided into two watches with orders to stand by the boats.

Down in a hold, Tom Beattie of the RAF had been playing cards and drinking. Suddenly, he started to vomit. So he climbed up on deck to get some air. A warrant officer collared him, and told him to stay there to act as a runner.

Returning with his family to their cabin after lunch, the Fairey manager, Legroux, suggested to his wife and children that they should put on their life belts. Doing so, they sat on their bunks waiting for the liner to move off.

In another cabin, Sisters Trott and Chamley of the Church Army, who had travelled to St-Nazaire in a military convoy which was attacked by German planes, were looking through a porthole when they saw a black cloud in the sky, moving very fast. It was a German plane homing in on the *Lancastria*.

Arriving in London at the end of their journey from Bordeaux, General Spears installed Charles de Gaulle in a small flat in Curzon Place in Mayfair, and then took him to lunch at the RAC Club in Pall Mall. In the early afternoon, they drove to Downing Street where Churchill was sitting in the sun in the garden of Number Ten.

De Gaulle was not Churchill's first choice to head the resistance to the Germans and the Pétain regime. A British mission had gone to Bordeaux to try to get Paul Reynaud or the former Interior Minister, Georges Mandel, to come to London to lead a government in exile. Mandel chose to sail to North Africa with other politicians who wanted to continue the fight from French possessions there – on arrival, he was arrested and held in German concentration camps until 1944 when he was handed over to the collaborationist militia in France and shot. Reynaud chose to stay in France. The following week, he was driving in the south of the country with his mistress when their car ran off the road. A suitcase in the back shot forward, hitting the Comtesse de Portes on the neck and killing her instantly. The former Premier was taken unconscious to hospital. When he recovered, he was arrested, sentenced to life imprisonment, and held prisoner in Germany throughout the war.

So the tall, gawky general, who was described by one senior British civil servant as having 'a head like a pineapple and hips like a woman', was the best candidate available, already displaying supreme self-confidence in his mission. Churchill greeted him in the Downing Street garden with a warm and friendly smile.

There was no concealing the gravity of the news, as Churchill acknowledged in a message to the British nation on 17 June. The defeat of the French army had turned into a rout. Officers abandoned their men, who headed home. In places, drunken troops commandeered any vehicles they could find, including ambulances. In Bordeaux, collaborationist politicians plotted in smart restaurants as they prepared to work with the Germans.

But, the Prime Minister insisted, what had happened in France made no difference to Britain's faith and purpose. 'We shall defend our island and, with the British Empire around us,' he declared, 'we shall fight on unconquerable until the curse of Hitler is lifted from the brows of men. We are sure that in the end all will be well.'[4]

The JU-88 was the pride of the Luftwaffe, having only come into service in 1939. It had angled wings and a complicated hydraulic system. Able to dive at 425 miles an hour, it could carry 6600 lbs of bombs, and was armed with four cannons as well as twin machine guns. The fully glazed nose provided the pilot with 180 degree vision. A Plexiglas panel below his seat improved the view as he swooped on the target. The plane was renowned for its steadiness as it dived – and the release of the bombs was accompanied by a howl from a hooter attached to the altimeter.

The crews chosen to man the JU-88s were an elite group. Peter Stahl, the former test pilot who had been among the first to fly them, was 'as proud as anything' to have been picked for the job. The four-man team consisted of a pilot, bomb aimer/navigator, wireless operator and gunner. The pilot could operate all commands from his seat, and fly single-handedly if necessary. With all the controls around him, Stahl felt like an organ player. The plane, he wrote in his diary, was 'almost like a temperamental star or diva: the JU-88 seems to know that it is beautiful and interesting, and behaves accordingly'.[5]

Approaching the west coast of France in the afternoon of 17 June, the pilots of the Junkers set the propeller blades at the best pitch, switched on the auxiliary fuel pumps, shut the radiator flaps, adjusted the altimeter, and fixed the contacts for the moment when they would pull out of their dive at an altitude of 2500 feet. The radio operators clicked the electric power to set the bomb fuses, and readied the automatic release gear. The crews checked their harness belts. The pilots rotated the trimming wheel to the diving marks, and activated the reflector sight to regulate the brightness of the aiming circle.

Below him, Stahl saw a large fleet of ships of all sizes in the wide estuary of the Loire. Furious anti-aircraft fire came up from the ground as he lay back from the main pack of Junkers to prepare his final approach. French single-engined Morane fighters flew in to attack them – a plane from another German squadron was hit, going down with its port engine on fire. A British Hurricane fighter piloted by 20-year-old Norman Hancock, who would later become a wing commander, followed one JU-88 for a long way, firing at it but not scoring a hit.

The dive-bombing technique which Stahl and the others had learned in training had been refined in the reality of war. The pilot throttled back the engine until it was almost idling; then he pulled the levers to activate the hydraulic dive brakes, at the same time setting the adjustable tailplane to such an acute angle that the plane dipped its nose with a jerk. The next moment, the JU-88 would shoot down towards the targets which grew larger in the sights as the pilot corrected the diving angle, looking upwards while he did so because that was now where the horizon was.

As Stahl prepared to dive, a Morane appeared 500 yards away. The German tipped the nose of his plane, and increased his speed. The French fighter followed. Dropping towards the ships strung out below him, Stahl decided to complete his bombing mission despite the enemy plane on his tail.

When the attack on the *Oronsay* ended, Captain Sharp and Chief Officer Grattidge had gone down to their cabins. It was 3.40 p.m. Grattidge had had no leave since the start of the war, and just wanted to get some rest. But he could not nod off. He felt a sense of impending disaster, got off his bunk and looked at his watch – it showed 3.44. A minute later, the siren on the ship sounded.

Grattidge stood in his cabin listening to the 'longest and most fearful silence' he had ever heard. Then, there was the noise of the bomb coming so fast that it ripped at his eardrums – a 'chilling banshee scream . . . howling from the sky'.[6]

The attack missed. Men packed tightly on the deck jeered as the explosions sent up huge columns of water, but caused no damage to the liner. Sidney Dunmall and his colleagues from the Pay Corps laughed their heads off. 'They couldn't hit us if they tried,' they called out. They were, he recalled, 'sublimely confident, couldn't care less, just happy to be going home'.

Then Dunmall heard that bars of chocolate were being distributed from the Purser's office, so he went down below to join a long queue waiting for the hand-outs. As he moved towards the front of the line outside the Purser's office, he had a premonition. Get out, get out, it told him. Though there were only two men still in front of him, he hurried up the stairs of the companionway.

In the dining room, a gunner from the City of London Regiment was sitting at a table talking to comrades when he heard the whistle of a falling bomb followed by a thud. They looked at one another, not knowing what to do. 'It's all right, that one went over the side,' a crew member shouted. The soldiers breathed a sigh of relief, and tried to make conversation. On the upper deck, an army officer brandished his pistol at men sitting there to make them go down below for safety's sake in case there was another attack.

Hearing the siren, Rudolph Sharp hurried to the bridge, where Grattidge joined him. At the end of the stern, Captain Field of the Army Medical Corps, who had been lying on the deck using his life jacket as a pillow while he read a book, felt sick with dread as he watched the German bomber climbing back up into the sky. Other Luftwaffe planes were arriving, flying in from the north-east. Field could sense how vulnerable the *Lancastria* was, with its lack of serious gun power.

Down in the sixteen-foot-high, Italianate dining room, with its arches, columns and ivory walls, Clement Stott, the Welshman who wore a pince-nez, felt no fear. The steward had just served his table with a selection of liqueurs to round off lunch when there was a tremendous crash. The steward went outside, and returned to assure everybody that the *Lancastria* had not been hit. Finishing his drink, the Welsh accountant went to his cabin, lay on his bunk and, comfortably full of food and drink, immediately fell asleep.

With the French Morane fighter still on his tail, Peter Stahl raised his speed as he prepared to dive, his sights set on what he described as 'a fat freighter'. Like the other JU-88s swooping on the evacuation fleet, he had the sun behind him to blind the gunners below. Homing in on the target, he pulled up the plane's nose a bit. A blast from the hooter connected to the altimeter signalled that he was at the correct height. With a light push on a red button on the control column, he released the bombs.

Six planes were diving on the estuary. Men on the ship's top deck ducked as they swooped so low that they could see the faces of the pilots.

Nineteen-year-old Henry Harding had gone down to the canteen to get a bottle of beer, but found it too hot in the queue. So he climbed to the top deck, and stretched out, resting his head on the life jacket he had been given when coming on board. Looking up, he saw two rotating propellers and bombs dropping.

There was a chatter of guns, and somebody shouted hopefully, 'Got the bastard.' But, this time, the *Lancastria* was hit by four high explosive bombs.

They landed with an impact which Captain Field described as being 'like someone bursting a child's tin kettle drum with a hammer'. Three blew up in the holds, instantly killing many of those who had been sent below decks for safety's sake, including the 800 RAF men crowded in one space. The fourth bomb either fell down the funnel or landed right beside it – Sharp thought that it was the first, but others who were in the engine room at the time said this could not have been the case or they would not have survived.

Bodies flew high in the air. Fires flared fore and aft, sending up an enormous cloud of black smoke. The air reeked of cordite. The starboard half of the liner's signal yard was destroyed, and the rigging hung slack.

Scalding steam belched from burst pipes, sometimes on to men packed so tightly in passages that they could not move. Water poured in through holes that the explosions had punched in the hull. Ropes were thrown down into flooded holds, but there were too few for the hundreds trapped below.

In the ship's hospital, a blast killed all twelve people in a bay. One of the bombs hit a bulkhead and ripped open an oil tank, unleashing 1400 tons of fuel. Big splinters of wood from the walls and floors impaled people standing nearby. A padre was trapped when a bomb sliced through the roof and side wall of his cabin: the damage jammed the door so tightly that nobody could get in to save him.

In the ornate dining room, Fernande Tips saw 'a sort of shadow' as the bombs fell. Then a mass of splinters flew through the air. Something hit her hard in one eye, and there was a tremendous bang. Crockery crashed from the tables. Chairs slid crazily across the floor through the smoke and fumes. In the bar, a Major had just poured whiskies and sodas for himself and his commanding officer when the explosion sent the glasses flying from their hands.

Seeing the bombs dropping from the Junkers, Henry

Harding quickly plotted their course, and realised that the ship would be hit. Burying his head in his life jacket, he heard everything go suddenly quiet – then there was pandemonium.

As Harding jumped up, a steward in the Cunard livery came up to him.

'It's all right son,' he said. 'this is a good ship, it isn't going to sink.'

'You may think it isn't going to sink,' Harding replied. 'I have my own ideas and I'm going to get off.' He pulled on his life jacket, and jumped into the sea. His watch stopped at 4.10 p.m.

CHAPTER 6

The Sinking

WITHIN TWO MINUTES of being bombed, the *Lancastria* was listing heavily. Ships around her fired their guns, but, though one Stuka trailed smoke, most of the shells burst too low.

Edwin Quittenton of the Royal Engineers, who had been sent to a hold deep in the ship, had snatched some sleep, and had then set out to climb to the top deck with a friend to take the air. On the way, they had passed hundreds of sleeping soldiers.

In the crush by the bar, Quittenton had looked round for his friend and had just located him when there was a crash. His friend disappeared. The boat listed. The lights went out. Edwin felt a hot draught, and something hit him on the head. 'It was hell let loose,' he recalled, 'a raging furnace.' The fumes made him feel sick as he groped about in the dark, stumbling over bodies. Moans and shouts came from all round him. 'This is my lot,' he mumbled to himself, and then, 'No, dammit, there must be a way out!'

In the French Renaissance-style main lounge, with its oak panels and barrel-vaulted ceiling, a seething mass of men fought to escape up the staircase. Some smashed the leaded windows to make their way on to the deck. An army chaplain standing by the staircase called out: 'Go steady there. There is plenty of time.'

Outside the lounge, a First World War veteran, who had served in the Battle of Passchendaele, stood to attention. When a fellow soldier asked if he would join him in trying to get to a lifeboat, the sergeant replied that he was waiting for the order to abandon ship.

A crew member was helped along a corridor, his face a mass of blood. He made no sound, calmed by shock. A sergeant, described by his captain as 'exceedingly stout', was trapped in his cabin, unable to push his way through the jammed, half-open door or to squeeze through the porthole. Seeing men panicking, a major in the Royal Engineers called out to them to remember that they were British.

On the top deck, an army sergeant from the Fire Service shouted: 'Come on lads; roll out the fire hoses.'

'You're wasting your time,' Donald Draycott told him.

William Henry Tilley, a Canadian soldier from Winnipeg, flung himself face down on the deck when the bombs exploded. Seconds later, he felt hot water thrown up from inside the ship on the back of his battledress.

Standing up, he saw the gaping hole in the upper deck, and tried to go below to help. But his path was blocked by injured men lying on the companionway. People were running round with blood streaming from their heads, some bleeding so profusely that they could not see where they were going.

Returning from his abandoned trip to collect chocolate from the Purser's office, Sidney Dunmall was blinded by a tremendous flash in front of him as he reached the top deck. Smoke billowed up. His hair and one arm were singed.

Looking round, he saw that the deck rail had gone, and the mast was broken. A man with a shattered arm cried out for help. Dunmall slithered down a rope to the sea. Round him were older soldiers from the Pioneer Corps hanging on to ropes and screaming, 'Save Me, Save Me, I can't swim.' Nor could Dunmall.

Men on the top deck were throwing planks as big as railway sleepers over the side to support those in the water. Sidney grabbed one, digging his nails into the wood. He hung on for grim death, until the man with a life belt pulled him clear of the sinking ship.

Harry Pettit of the RASC, who had worked on RAF airfields in eastern France before being evacuated across the country, shook hands with a friend called Charlie, and said: 'This is it; here we go.' Together, they dropped into the sea.

Sinking below the water, 24-year-old Harry felt as if his lungs were going to burst. The compression made him fear he was about to explode. The pressure on his ears was intense. A hundred things from the past flitted through his mind in a few seconds that seemed like hours. He conjured up a clear, calm picture of his home and his widowed mother, and wished that death by drowning did not take so long. Then his fall through the water was halted when he hit a sandbank, and shot up to the surface like a cork, gasping and choking on the oil he had swallowed.

*

Coming out the dive after dropping their bombs, the JU-88s jolted, and the gravitational force pinned the crew tightly back into their seats as they pressed their heads against the back rest to avoid them being thrown forwards on to their chests. For a few seconds, they lost consciousness while the planes shot upwards.

With the French fighter still on his tail, Peter Stahl did not look down to see where his bombs had fallen. He put his aircraft into a steep downward banking movement. The Morane followed, but was not catching up. Stahl executed a series of twists, and flew steeply upwards to gain space. The French pilot was still there behind him, steadying his course to fire. Stahl went into another bank. The two planes dodged across the sky, and then, suddenly, the fighter turned away and headed back for the estuary. Stahl set the Junkers on a homeward course.

'The encounter had been rather hairy to say the least,' he wrote in his diary.[1] But the KG30 planes got back to their base in Belgium without any losses, though one was hit more than seventy times and had to make a belly landing. Stahl noted that the unit had scored 'a number of good hits', even if the crews did not know exactly what their bombs had blasted.

Whether the 'fat freighter' Stahl mentioned as his target was, in fact, the *Lancastria* or whether he was aiming at another vessel cannot now be established. No boat among the evacuation fleet that was bombed appears to have corresponded exactly to that two-word description. Stahl was certainly among the pilots who swooped on ships in the estuary since his diary records that he did not fly in over the St-Nazaire harbour. Diving in so fast, he might well have taken the liner for a large freighter. But, if so, it will never be known if his Junker was the plane that made the first, unsuccessful dive on the liner or the second, which hit the *Lancastria.*

'God, look at those flames,' Captain Sharp said to Harry Grattidge as they stared from the bridge. Oil from the fuel tank had caught fire, sending up clouds of inky smoke. The deck was covered with blood and splintered woodwork. A screaming man, his face and hands scalded by steam, ran across in front of them and leaped into the sea.

Standing by the deck rail, Percy Braxton of the RAF heard a voice saying, 'There he is!' Two men were pointing over the starboard bow. For a moment, Braxton thought one of the German planes had gone into the sea. Looking over the side, he saw 'a large pit of red swirling water and a human head going round and round'. It was a man who had been blown through a hole in the liner's side.

On the top deck, crew members were pushing through hundreds of soldiers to try to lower the lifeboats. Some men had already climbed into one boat, and sat there as if expecting it to lower itself automatically to the sea. Soon, the craft was so crowded that there was only room to stand.

The chaplain, who had counselled calm in the lounge, took charge of the men round him on the deck. He told them to remove their boots, puttees and heavy clothing, and then to go over the side. Some leaped into the air; others slid down the side of the liner as it came up out of the water. The chaplain waited till they had all gone, then tried to follow. But the angle of the deck had become so acute that he could not make his way to the rail. He called to the last man on the rail to stick out his leg, grasped it and pulled himself up and over, sliding down into the sea.

Richard Newlove of the RASC was shaking hands with two friends before jumping into the sea when he heard a detonation behind him, and felt something rubbing against his back. He turned, and saw the body of a young officer who had just shot himself. A second young officer bent down, picked up the revolver and killed himself, too.

An elderly sailor and an RAF man lashed a rope on to a stanchion near the stern, and threw one end over the side. 'Down you go and when you reach the bottom put your feet to the side of the ship and give a good kick outwards,' they told the men around them. Percy Braxton nodded at the old man to go ahead of him, but he replied, 'No, ye go laddie.' So Braxton took off his boots, threw his tin helmet on the deck and climbed down the rope. He watched the propellers rising in the sky above him, kicked off the side of the ship and fell into the water.

Stan Flowers and his fellow townsman from Faversham, Wally Smith, from the transport unit at St-Etienne-de-Montluc, had been in a hold when the bombs exploded. Aged twenty and twenty-one respectively, they managed to get up to the deck though the rail of the stairway they used collapsed under them. At first, there was panic. Then they calmed down as they found themselves on the high part of the ship, with a long drop down to the sea. They removed their boots, putting them down neatly one beside the other. Shaking hands, they grabbed ropes hanging over the side. As they slid down, the chaffing badly burned their hands.

Both went under the surface, but they came up together and swam more vigorously than they ever had in their lives to get away from the sinking liner. Finding two floating deck chairs, they draped themselves over them. There were massive jellyfish in the water round them. From time to time, they shouted abuse up at the German planes. But the movement of the water separated the two men, and they were too tired to be able to make the effort to keep together. They never saw one another again.

When soldiers came to the bridge, Captain Sharp tried to reassure them, but he knew that there were only 2000 life belts on board for three times that many men. Signallers called into the intercom to tell the dozen men in the engine room to evacuate. Despite the shock of the bombing, the electrician, Frank Brodgen, who was on duty there, recalled that they took their time to leave, getting their things together and checking that everybody was present before they went up through the hatch, urging soldiers they saw to follow them.

Grattidge and Sharp looked at one another, saying nothing. The Chief Officer felt as if he was at a deathbed. But he had to take action. Picking up a megaphone, he called out: 'Clear away the boats now. Your attention, please . . . clear away the boats.'

When the liner listed to starboard, Grattidge shouted through the megaphone for men on the deck to go over to the port side to try to balance her. As he issued his order, he saw the ship's Second Officer standing in front of him with a sheaf of papers in one hand while he tugged up his trousers with the other – he had been dressing when the bombs landed. Despite the death and chaos all around, Grattidge could not stop himself laughing.

The Chief Officer's instruction had a temporary effect in

righting the ship. But then she listed too far to port, her deck dropping towards the water, her stern rising in the air. At the very back of the liner, Captain Field sat 'perched like a bird' watching the crowd below him struggling to release the ropes holding the lifeboats. Sailors were throwing everything that floated over the side for those already in the water, but the tide carried most of it away.

Field saw 'bodies and oil, bodies some with their life jackets on.' Good swimmers forged through the water, one still wearing his helmet. Closer at hand, 'decks were packed with soldiers laden with rifles and equipment, just waiting for a miracle to happen'. A man dived from the deck clad only in his underpants.

'Off with your boots, and over the side!' Harry Grattidge called. Men sat down on the listing deck to do so; some stripped completely to make swimming easier. Thomas Hutchison, a 19-year-old soldier from the Number One Heavy Repair Shop, started to comply with the Chief Officer's order, but he could not undo the laces on one boot. So he jumped into the water still wearing it. He lay on his back in the sea as German planes came in to strafe. Deciding that, if he was going to be killed, he was not going to watch it happen, he rolled on to his side. The bullets missed him by inches.

A Welsh soldier, Peter Lawrence, who had been burned on his face and arms, took a life jacket from a corpse and jumped when the deck was six feet from the surface of the sea. 'Goodbye,' a friend called out. 'See you later, best of luck.' Lawrence turned on to his back, and flapped his arms to get himself moving away from the liner.

More German planes swept in to drop flares and to strafe the ship, their bullets crackling like hail. Captain Field decided it was time to leave his vantage point at the end of the stern where he risked being sucked down with the ship. Before making the seventy-foot drop into the sea, he took all his money out of the pocket of his trousers and lodged it behind a hatch cover. It was, he later reflected, 'a sign of how we go a bit mad under the strain'.

From the cliffs overlooking the estuary, the air force wireless operator, Vic Flowers, and the other two RAF men, who had got back across the gangway of the tender in the harbour, saw German aircraft skimming over their heads. Then they heard explosions on the sea below. Smoke soon obscured their view of the sinking of the ship they had refused to board. Flowers was later told that thirty-seven of his ground crew group died on the *Lancastria*.

On the ship, survival could be a matter of chance or of where you were – those on the top deck had the best chance. Those down below who were fortunate enough to be near portholes or hold doors scrambled through them – one sergeant pushed a little brown dog out in front of him.

Having a life jacket could be a double-edged privilege. Men jumping into the water wearing one were strangled or had their necks broken by the stiff cork collars. The place you chose to sit could make the difference between life and death. As the bombs hit, the Sherwood Forester, G. Skelton, was turning to talk to his friend, Joe Saxton, for whom he was looking after the picture of his girlfriend. Joe simply wasn't there any more: he had been blown away by the blast. Skelton was only wounded in the right shoulder.

Just before the attack, a sergeant major from the RASC had returned to the stateroom where he was billeted and told his colleagues of the excellent 'posh feed' lunch he had just enjoyed in the dining room. The others hurried off to eat. It was the last he saw of them.

Another RASC soldier was sent by his cabin mates to fetch beer. While he was waiting in line to be served, the first bombs fell outside the ship. Water and fish flowed in through the open porthole. Still, the soldier went ahead and bought three bottles of Bass, returning to his cabin. The beer drunk, he went out on to the deck to put the bottles in a refuse bin. He was not harmed when the bombs exploded in the lower part of the ship.

Down below, one man walked on a carpet of the dead in the passages as he sought an escape route. Reaching the top of the ship, he linked up with another soldier, and they slid together down the almost vertical deck, stood on the rail and walked off into the water. They never saw one another again.

In the lounge, the weight of men struggling to get up from the lower decks broke the rail of the main stairway, sending dozens falling down on those below. Then the whole stairway collapsed, cutting off escape.

Sid Keenan and his friend, John Broadbent, who had gone into a bathroom marked 'Officers Only', were shaving and washing when the alarm sounded for the second attack. They heard a terrible crash, and everything seemed to shudder. 'I bet nobody ever left a bath quicker than I,' Broadbent recalled. 'When Sid and I got back on deck, it was a case of every man for himself.'

Major Scott-Bowden was resting in his cabin when the

bombs hit. He picked up his rubber boots containing the bottles of whisky and mineral water and linked by a piece of string. He hung them round his neck, and went on to the deck in his bare feet. As the ship tilted, he grabbed the handle of a door which opened – on the other side, he saw iron staircases coming up from the engine room full of climbing men. He took the bottles from his boots, put them down and pulled on the boots before jumping into the sea.

Norman Driver was in a toilet. Burning timber fell on him. His pal, Cal Beal from Sheffield, shouted from an adjoining lavatory, 'I've been hit. There's blood on my leg.' In fact, he had not been injured, but had pulled up his trousers so fast in the shock of the explosions that he had wet them and, in the panic of the moment, had taken the stain for blood. Opening the toilet door, Driver looked at the spot where another of his group, Londoner George Watling, had been having a wash and shave. There was a hole in the floor. Watling was not seen again.

With Beal holding on to him, Driver made his way up a gangway to a loading bay running the full width of the ship. Men and their kit were sliding down the sharply tilting deck. Seeing light from the doors above, Norman and Cal scrambled out on to the deck. Beal put a cigarette in his mouth, lit it – and then they both jumped into the sea. As they went under the water, they lost contact with one another. When he came up, Cal tried to puff at his sodden cigarette. Norman hit his head on a life raft as he surfaced, but managed to swim to a lifeboat and was pulled on board.

Men from the Church Army and YMCA kneeled on the deck in prayer before getting up to help non-swimmers. One young padre holding a Bible went below to comfort men. A sailor warned him of the danger. 'I know,' he replied. 'But those men need God. They are my people.' He did not survive.

The padre, Charles McMenemy, who had served as Catholic chaplain at Wormwood Scrubs prison before the war, also went below and led a group of men to a loading port six feet above the water. He gave his life belt to a sergeant major who could not swim, waiting till all the men were in the water before he jumped.

In the passageways, men cleared a path for Mrs Tillyer and her two-year-old daughter. As the mother and child passed, they stood back, delaying their own escape until they saw the pair was safely out on deck.

In his cabin, Clement Stott was awakened from his postprandial nap by the bombs. The door flew open, and a man covered in blood fell through it. Getting outside, the Captain saw a dignified grey-haired woman sliding down the deck, screaming as she went.

As an accountant steeped in the importance of numbers, Stott tried to carry out a roll call of his unit. This proved difficult in the circumstances. When he called the names of two corporals, he was told that they had been killed. Stott instructed his men that they would be safer staying with him than jumping into the sea. The steepness of the ship's list meant that people leaping from the superstructure were crashing into the hull or hitting the edges of portholes, screaming as they died in a mass of blood and broken heads.

Stott took off his pince-nez, and put it in its case. 'I knew I should need my glasses when I got ashore,' he recalled. 'But I knew even more that it would have a good steadying effect if the men could see I wasn't in a panic.'

Then he stood to attention, and called out as if on a parade ground: 'Detachment, 67th Company. Detachment! Abandon ship! Follow me, boys, and good luck!'

'Good luck, Sir!' the soldiers shouted back.

The Captain climbed the deck rail, stepped on to the side of the ship and moved towards the sea, followed by his men. Water was lapping over the hull. Stott asked a ship's officer if he should remove his boots. Yes, the man shouted. So the Captain sat down, and began to undo the laces. But then he thought that he would need his boots when he got to dry land, just as he would need his pince-nez. Though they might hamper him in the water, he decided to keep them on.

As he sat on the hull, Stott saw a man trying to squeeze through a porthole, but he was wearing so much webbing equipment that he was stuck.

'Cut your straps!' Stott shouted to him. A wave hit the porthole, and the man disappeared. Another soldier dived through it, naked except for his army identity tags.

Suddenly Stott found himself sinking beneath the sea. As he rose back to the surface, he found that a man was hanging on to his feet.

'I realised I had to get rid of him quick, or we'd both drown,' the Captain recalled. 'I kicked hard and struggled free of him. Sticking to heavy army boots had paid off already!'

Fernande Tips tried to keep with her family as they fled from the dining room. But they became separated as they went up the stairway to the deck. Clifford Tillyer saw his wife and daughter into a lifeboat, and soldiers pushed him in after them. As the boat was lowered, its ropes jammed in the davits.

It tilted over, throwing the occupants into the water and separating the Tillyers. A man holding on to a piece of wood gave it to Mrs Tillyer and Jacqueline. As they floated away, the mother kept calling out 'Baby here,' 'Baby here.' After a while Jacqueline picked up the two words, and repeated the sounds until she became too weak to make any noise.

The Fairey manager, Legroux, took his 13-year-old daughter, Emilie, by the hand while Madame Legroux led their 11-year-old son, Roger, towards the lifeboats. They were all wearing life jackets.

'The stairs weren't straight as they should be,' Roger remembered. 'There was panic on board, people were shrieking and shouting, guns were firing at German planes, it was chaos.'

When they got to a lifeboat, it was packed. People were jumping all over the place. His mother and sister got in. His father threw Roger into the boat; then climbed in himself.

As they waited for the boat to be lowered, soldiers jumped in and the craft became unbalanced. One side tilted. Everybody fell out. As he dropped, Roger was holding his father by the hand. On the way down, he let go.

The boy sank below the oil-covered water. When he came back to the surface, his mother was next to him. Roger clung to her and to Fernande Tips, who had ended up in the water near the Legroux family. Around him, he saw soldiers all over the place, and heard hundreds of voices singing 'Roll Out the Barrel'. Then Roger passed out because of the amount of water and oil he had swallowed. The two women kept his head above the sea.

His sister was floating in a different part of the sea. Emilie was worried because she had lost a pair of wonderful red shoes her father had bought for her. Soon, she found herself riding on a man's back. She thought he was her father. She ran her hands over him, and she may have screamed when she realised he was a stranger.

Some soldiers passing by on a raft took the girl on board. From there, she saw her mother and brother about a hundred yards away. Three members of the Legroux family were safe, but their father was lost for ever.

Michael Sheehan, of the *Lancastria* crew, was thrown along a passageway by the force of the first bombs that missed the liner. He got up on deck by the time of the second attack. Reaching the fore deck, he pulled off all his clothes, and dived into the sea, where he found a hatch board. Two soldiers were already hanging on to it. Together, they struck out from the sinking ship, but both soldiers were killed by strafing, and Sheehan was left alone, covered with oil.

Joe Sweeney was lying down in a smoking room when the bombs exploded. Going to the door, he saw a demented soldier swinging his rifle round and round over his head, cursing and swearing. After the butt of the gun hit somebody on the head, a man rugby-tackled the crazed figure.

The lights went out; the uproar grew louder. Water began to trickle down the companionway, and then gushed on the stairs. Bells clanged amid the screams. Some people began to sing military, religious and patriotic airs.

Sweeney got out on the deck, took off his jacket, and hopped over the deck rail. He left behind the chalice from the clergyman's briefcase and his cache of Players cigarettes he had stowed behind a ventilator vent.

The tilt of the ship meant he landed on the side of the hull, bruising and scratching himself. For a while, he sat there, smoking a cigarette handed to him by an old soldier. The two men discussed if it was better to be clothed or naked to survive in the sea. Sweeney removed his trousers, and slid into the water.

He went under. As he rose to the surface, he was grabbed round the neck by somebody shouting 'I can't swim' and pulling them both under again. Struggling free from the other man's grasp, Sweeney rose to the surface again and clung on to a plank with two other men – a fourth person lay across it. Together they floated away from the *Lancastria*.

In the chaos and darkness below decks, Edwin Quittenton groped along a wall. Suddenly, he felt a flap in the wall beside him give way, letting in a streak of light. He pushed at the flap, and got a glimpse of an empty open porthole. Followed by other men, he began to climb through it, but got stuck.

He felt as if he was in the jaws of a trap, the water immediately beneath him, men shouting from behind for him to get through the opening. When he did not move, they started to push him, but the more pressure they exerted, the tighter his body became rammed in the porthole.

'I can't move!' Quittenton shouted. 'Pull me back inside.'

At last they did so, and slimmer men swarmed through the porthole as fast as they could. Quittenton saw another porthole, and opened it to let in more light. Looking round, he spotted a wooden door which might provide an escape route. It was locked, so he kicked it down. On the other side lay an iron door in the hull. He unscrewed the bolts on it, but the 45 degree angle at which the *Lancastria* was listing made it impossible to lift the door open on his own.

He could hear men talking behind him 'in all kinds of babble', and he called for them to help him. Pushing together, they soon had the door open. Below lay the sea. Quittenton could not swim, but he saw a dangling rope, and launched himself into the air to grab it. Going under after jumping from the hull, he swallowed too much water for comfort. But, coming to the surface, he saw a lifeboat only a few feet away and got to it by kicking out.

Joe O'Brien, the teenage waiter on the *Lancastria* who had been called back from the pub in Liverpool three days earlier, was in the dining room when the bombs hit. Using his knowledge of the liner's lay-out and her passageways, he got up to the promenade deck, bypassing corridors full of men screaming as boiling water sprayed on them from broken pipes.

Reaching the top of the ship, Joe found himself jammed up against a deck rail by the press from behind him. He climbed over, and held on the outside. Beside him, he saw the big figure of the liner's chef, Joe Pearse, who had promised his father to look after him. A steward, Johnny Rock, from Glasgow, was also there. They all had life jackets.

'Come on, Joe, get in,' Rock shouted, giving the youth a push.

The trip down to the sea was, O'Brien recalled, 'like coming down from the Empire State Building'. He remembered the drill for the cork and canvas life jackets. 'When you hit the sea, the jacket stops, but your body goes on falling. So you risk having your neck broken. To prevent that, put your knees up and tug the jacket down.'

By applying the drill, O'Brien saved himself from joining those who had not been told it and died as a result. Dropping below the surface, he thought he would never come up. But then he shot out, and swam away as strongly as he could. His protector, Joe Pearse, failed to follow the drill, and broke his neck. Johnny Rock survived.

The two Church Army sisters, who had seen the bomber flying down on the *Lancastria* like a black cloud, got into a lifeboat. While it was being lowered, it tilted as the liner keeled over. One end lodged against the hull, and then hit a porthole. Hearing soldiers calling for help, the sisters handed over their life belts. Then, their boat swung free, and went down the rest of the way, the great bulk of the *Lancastria* looming above them.

Captain Brooke of the Pay Corps slipped into the sea though he had never learned to swim. But he vowed that Hitler was not going to deprive his wife and family of his company, nor stop him enjoying the pension he had earned with service stretching back more than twenty-one years. Once in the water, he found, to his surprise, that he could swim after all.

J. H. Drummond of the RAF had been lying down after a 'lovely hot bath' when the bulkhead in front of him erupted in a huge sheet of flame, and he was blown upside down against a wall. He felt his hair on fire – his face had also been flashburned though he did not realise this immediately.

In utter darkness, Drummond struggled to his feet. He

could not breathe; the blast had blown all the oxygen out of the room. He stretched his mouth to its limit as he gasped to get air in his lungs. Eventually he succeeded.

He lost his bearings in the dark, but heard someone grunting and sobbing nearby. Reaching the other man, he asked if there was a way out.

'Please push me up,' the man said.

Drummond did so, and someone behind them said there was an escape ahead. Drummond tried to climb up, himself; but all he could feel in front of him was a huge flat sheet of metal.

Sinking down, utterly exhausted, he felt he was finished. Everything was quiet. He could not hear anybody else near him. He thought of his father, who had been killed in the First World War, and of the tough life his mother had had as a war widow. That must not happen to his wife, Marjorie, he decided.

'Then I thought, if I had unwittingly harmed anybody, now it is up to God to decide,' he recalled.

All of a sudden, a voice behind him asked: 'Is there any way out?'

'Yes, give me a push up,' Drummond replied.

As he went up, he could feel the edge of the sheet of metal. A very faint glimmer came from far above. Crawling on, he got to some stairs. Ahead, along a corridor, a dim light filtered from a broken-down cabin door. Behind it was a mass of wire like a huge spider's web.

Despite the danger of electrocution, Drummond dived through the wire. He ran along a corridor, seeing daylight at the end. Water began to run down the floor. Two men who had got out of the hold before him were trying to escape through a porthole. He did not stop to join them, rushing on wildly towards the daylight coming through an open loading port. Reaching his destination, he found a warrant officer standing there. The man gave Drummond a cigarette and a light, and he stood staring silently into the sea. Then the warrant officer said, 'Better get in lad – there's a lot of stuff on the top deck will be toppling over soon.' Drummond jumped.

Amid the chaos, some kept calm, taking off their uniforms, and folding them neatly before leaping into the sea. The blast blew all the clothes off one man, leaving him in his boots and socks. Two men with badly burned arms took off their clothes, but put on tin helmets to protect their heads from the strafing. An interpreter stripped down to a pair of blue silk swimming trunks which he had bought in La Baule.

John Broadbent, who had been in the 'Officers Only' bath when the bombs fell, did not bother to put on his clothes before running out and jumping into the sea. Padre McMenemy gave his blue Lilo to two soldiers who did not know how to swim. On the top deck, a lance corporal came across a second lieutenant and four men crying. They had no life jackets, and could not swim. So the lance corporal helped to tear up some wooden boxes to give them something to cling on to when they went into the water.

Sitting on the side of the liner as she listed more and more steeply, Alec Cuthbert found himself sliding down the hull as far as the propeller – he had never realised how huge it was, 'as big as a house'. He waited till the water reached his feet, and then walked out into the sea.

Peter Vinicombe, the RAF man from the Scottish Borders who had been so impressed by the size of the *Lancastria* that morning, had been blown off his feet by the blast that came up through a hatch to the deck space by the funnel where he was standing. He landed in the lap of an army officer sitting nearby with several other soldiers. Another explosion went off, and the officer and his men ran away, kicking Vinicombe in the face as they did so.

Army kit was scattered all round him. People hurtled down the deck and over the rails. Unable to swim, Vinicombe scrambled for a safer place on the ship, watching as the masts came down parallel to the water. Men were walking before jumping. Seeing the propellers sticking up in the air, Vinicombe realised that the liner was now upside down, and that he was sitting on the keel.

As a big oily wave washed towards him, he grabbed at a rope, losing his footing and falling into the sea. When he came to the surface, he took hold of two floating kitbags, and then found an oar from a lifeboat. With the oar between his legs and a kitbag under each arm, he floated free of the liner.

Lieutenant Colonel Norman de Coudray Tronson, the veteran of three wars, got out on to the fore deck and helped fire a Bren gun at the German planes. As the liner sank deeper, a wave washed him overboard.

Ginger-haired Stanley Rimmer, whose life had been saved by the advice from his naval brother not to stay below, clung on to a pipe as the ship listed, though its heat burned his hands. Getting into the water without a life belt, he ducked repeatedly below the surface to avoid bullets from German planes. Then he saw two corpses wearing life jackets. He put an arm over each body and floated between them. As he did so, a man wearing a greatcoat jumped from the deck and landed beside him, calling out 'Mother! Mother!'

*

Men from the Motor Transport detachment, which had been delayed boarding by the overloaded RAF contingent, had set up three Bren guns on the boat deck as soon as they had got on the ship. Because it was a warm day, they were in short sleeves. Their unit's report said that they were 'the only ones complete with tripods ammunition etc'.[2]

It was hard to see the German planes flying in out of the sun. One of the guns, manned by Lance Corporal Fred Coe, the former boy soldier from Bury St Edmunds, was hit and damaged by machine-gun fire from a plane. 'The aircraft were very noisy,' he recalled. 'By the time you sighted them they were gone; they were so quick – bombed from low level, just a few hundred feet.'

Looking down the deck, Coe saw a screaming, bleeding soldier running to the side and taking off his helmet before he jumped into the sea. He heard Harry Grattidge's instruction to run to the other side to balance the ship. Then a sergeant told him 'Take your boots off, boy' – which he did, handing his damaged Bren gun to the other man as he unlaced them. But he could see that it was useless – the ship was going to go down.

So Fred and a friend decided it was time to leave. As they walked to the side, they saw five soldiers crying as they stood up to their knees in water. They could not swim. Coe and his colleague fetched a wooden box for them, then swam off the ship over the submerged rail.

On the top deck, Morris Lashbrook and his friend, 'Chippy' Moore, were manning another Bren gun as the bombs landed. When Morris recovered from the blast, the gun was gone. An officer in a black beret told them to go to the other side of the ship to join in the attempt to balance her. When that proved fruitless, the officer told them: 'I think you chaps had better get off down the side.' So they stripped and climbed down ropes to the sea.

One of the Bren gunners was killed, his finger still on the trigger. Another had his arm blown off. An army private grabbed a gun and fired at the planes until a lump of flying debris hit him on the head and knocked him out. Revived by a corporal, the private refused to leave, continuing to fire as the sea lapped at his feet. By 4.08, the gunners were shin deep in water, and the angle of the deck made it impossible to keep the Bren guns in position. So they took to the sea, singing 'Roll Out the Barrel'.

As the liner dropped ever lower in the water, surrounded by whirlpools that dragged down men and debris, Sergeant Major Picken of the RASC watched one of his men, a private who had got married just before going to France, standing transfixed, staring down at the sea. Picken tried to get him to move, but the young man just stood still and sobbed.

Picken, who had sheltered from German planes the previous night in a barrel in St-Nazaire, could not swim, and hesitated to leave the ship. But a corporal from his unit persuaded him that he might as well take his chance in the sea as stay where he was. So Picken and the corporal took off their jackets, trousers, shoes, socks and underpants, ready to go into the water. At that moment, an army nurse came up from a companionway. Embarrassed, Picken turned away from her. 'No need for modesty at a time like this,' she said with a firm smile.

Picken folded his clothes into a neat pile. He and the corporal stood facing one another.

'Good luck,' said the Sergeant Major.

'Same to you,' the other man replied.

They shook hands.

Behind them a cockney soldier said: 'That's all right. It ain't far to land. Only about a mile – straight down.'

The two men clutched a rope.

'Good luck,' they each cried as they slid down, the rope ripping the skin from their hands and legs as they went.

In the water Picken found a big floating duffel bag, and tucked it under his arm. He paddled and kicked with his feet to get away from the *Lancastria*, but the duffel bag was becoming waterlogged, and would soon sink.

He watched the planes coming in low over the sea, and the destroyer, *Highlander*, circling with its guns blazing up into the sky. Over his shoulder, Picken looked back at the liner, her keel covered with figures – like black dots or flies, said another man. Her stern rose higher in the air. The water had put out most of the fires on board, but there was still a pall of smoke over her. An officer stood on the hull calmly smoking a cigarette. The propeller screws jutting up against the sky began to dip. About fifty men still clung to them. They were singing, too:

> *There'll always be an England*
> *Where there's a country lane*
> *As long as there's a cottage small*
> *Beside a field of grain.*

At their base in Belgium, the Diving Eagle crews heard of France's capitulation. They were, Peter Stahl wrote, 'over the moon with joy'.[3] The local Belgians seemed to feel the same because they believed this meant that the war was over.

The Luftwaffe pilots staged a celebration that night, but, as the first impact of the French surrender wore off, their rejoicing was dampened by uncertainty about what would come next. Was the war now over, or would Britain go on fighting alone? What would that mean for Germany and its air force, which Hitler was counting on to shatter resistance across the Channel?

What did the Führer plan to do?

On the bridge of the *Lancastria*, Captain Sharp turned to his Chief Officer, and said: 'It's time now, Harry. I'm going to swim for the after-end.'

There was only one life belt to hand. Grattidge was a strong swimmer – he had won medals in races as a schoolboy in Stafford. Knowing that the Captain was a poor swimmer, the Chief Officer insisted that he take it.

'Good luck, Sir,' he said as Sharp did so.

The Captain dropped away into the water.

The sea was now very close, lapping like bathwater. Leaving behind the clothes in his cabin, his personal sextant, his camera, diaries, letters from his mother, a collection of penguins made of porcelain, metal and glass, and a copy of one of his favourite books, H. G. Wells' *Outline of History*, the Chief Officer waited till the floor of the bridge reached the surface. The great liner quaked once, as if in a final gesture of farewell. In his gold-braided Cunard Line uniform and a tin helmet, Harry Grattidge walked out into the sea.

CHAPTER 7

———

The Sea

THE *LANCASTRIA*'S STERN STOOD OUT against the sky like a sharp rock. Floating in the sea, John Broadbent saw a face behind a porthole. The terror-stricken man tried to smash the glass, but it was too thick. Before long, the porthole slid beneath the water.

The Canadian, William Tilley, who had jumped feet first, was passed by a man who told him, 'This will be worth a pint at my local when I get back to Wigan.'

A Hurricane fighter flew in with the sun behind it to attack a German plane machine-gunning men in the water. John Edwards, the interpreter who had dived into the sea in his blue swimming trunks, saw the British pilot waving as he swooped to 100 feet above the surface. Having hit the enemy aircraft, the Hurricane flew off – its pilot is believed to have been a 26-year-old Scot, George Berry, who would die in the Battle of Britain.

A survivor reported seeing the Luftwaffe plane floating in the water fifty yards from him. The crew stood on the wing as men from the *Lancastria* shouted 'Murder the bastards!' But one of the Germans brandished a Luger pistol, and the British kept away until he was picked up by a Royal Navy destroyer.

After the planes had gone, everything went quiet. Somebody said, 'It's a lovely day tomorrow.' A man asked Alec Cuthbert if he could hang on to his life jacket, adding: 'I don't think I'll last much longer.' Cuthbert gestured to him to do so, and they drifted together on the strong tide towards the mouth of the Loire.

Looking back at the liner on which he had served, Joe O'Brien thought she resembled a giant whale covered with khaki, air force blue and white jackets. On the keel, the men kept on singing 'Roll Out the Barrel'. Several survivors said they sang 'lustily'. Then the sound of 'There'll Always Be an England' came across the water, and a hymn 'To Our Returning Home'. An officer pushed men into the water to make them abandon the dying ship. In the sea, they joked about it being a nice day for a swim. A Royal Engineers corporal on the hull removed his clothes, took a flag and wrapped it round his body before jumping off.

The oil that spread across the water was almost as thick as tar. It coated the eyes of those in the sea, and went down their throats to choke them. Their arms and bodies became so slippery that they could not be hauled on to the rafts and upturned lifeboats.

Captain Sharp, who floated away from the *Lancastria* in the kapok life jacket Harry Grattidge had given him, had asked for the surplus fuel to be taken off before leaving Britain, but there had been no time to do so. Later, he would put the high death toll down equally to the lack of life jackets and to the oil which, he wrote, 'proved to be fatal in the end'.[1]

Feeling the fuel creeping across his body like cold black syrup, Grattidge swam for clean water. As he did so, he saw the exhausted, staring face of a man beside him. Spitting out oil from his mouth, the Chief Officer grasped at the man's hair to drag him to safety. When they reached a clear patch, he saw that what he was holding was a severed head.

A little later, Grattidge's vision went, and he was afraid that he had been hit in the head by a strafing bullet. Then he realised his tin helmet had tipped forward to cover his eyes.

He made his way to a small man swimming nearby, and asked him how he was getting on. The man was completely naked. He glanced at the gold braid on the arm of the Chief Officer's uniform, and gave a look of disgust as he replied in a cockney accent: 'What's the good of hanging on under conditions like this. Eh? What's the good? I tell you I'm so fed up I've got a perishing good mind to sink.' When Grattidge urged him to hang on, the little fellow said that, if his mother had known before he was born that he was going to suffer like this, she would have drunk more gin.

At 4.12 p.m., less than twenty minutes after being hit, the *Lancastria* disappeared below the sea for good. The estuary was relatively shallow – twelve fathoms, or seventy-two feet – and she soon came to lie on the bottom. Her last resting place was at latitude 47.09N, longitude 2.20W.

There were screams from men on the hull as the water swallowed her. Hundreds were pulled under by the suction.

A Sherwood Forester who had perched on the highest point of the stern believed he was the last man off. In the water, drowning men pulled him down, but he freed himself and bobbed back up to the surface in his life belt.

'Quietly and gracefully she went under, and the waters stilled over her,' Edwin Quittenton recalled.

The only record of her end was made by a 30-year-old naval volunteer, Frank Clements, on the destroyer, the *Highlander*. Navy men were not allowed to take cameras on board, but, as a volunteer working in naval stores, Clements had managed to keep his with him. He had run out of film on the voyage to St-Nazaire, but got some from a man in the port in exchange for a pair of socks. Standing on the deck of the warship, he photographed the hull covered with men as the keel dropped inexorably into the sea.

Sergeant Major Picken had always been sceptical about religion, but now he prayed 'hard and fast' as he held on desperately to an oar that floated by him. The oil on the water seemed as heavy as tar, as thick and sticky as molasses. Another man took hold of the oar, saying he could swim no more. The two of them could barely keep their heads above the surface. Both felt dreadfully tired. German planes dived towards the stretch of sea where they were, dropping flares which flickered on the water. The aircraft came back to strafe, the bullets ripping past like red-hot pokers. They saw bombs falling, too, sending up great spouts of water that rained down dead fish.

Unable to swim or dive below the surface to avoid the bullets, Picken prayed still more intently. The man on the other end of the oar looked over his shoulder. Suddenly, two high spouts of water zipped closer. The other man screamed, 'Oh, my Christ.' A bullet went through his forehead, his hands slipped, and he sank to his death.

Two men swam past dragging an unconscious fellow between them – they invited Picken to hang on to the third man's legs, but he decided to stay with his oar. A life raft covered with soldiers and airmen singing 'Roll Out the Barrel' floated by; those in the water told them to shut up.

After swimming for an hour away from the ship, the Bren gunner, Fred Coe, lay on his back and watched three British fighters come over and chase four German planes away. Wearing nothing much except for their identification discs, and with oil sticking to their bodies, Coe and the men around him grew numb; but their attitude was simple – 'Every man for himself, got to take charge of Number One in these circumstances.'

A swimmer glided through the water as if at the seaside, talking to those around him as he passed. A soldier noticed his unit's mascot swimming by, a French dog they called Buller – the animal had followed him each day when he bicycled to collect the post. Men cried out for divine help; one of them noted later that 'there were no atheists within my hearing'.

The chaplain, who had taken charge of men on the deck and told them to leave the ship, floated with two other men, one of them badly wounded. Their only support was a boathook. After a time, they came across a single man hanging on to a plank. They persuaded him to swap it for their boathook, and draped the wounded fellow over the plank.

A lifeboat went round in circles, the soldiers rowing it

pulling in different directions until an Irishman took charge, swearing at the men to make them coordinate their efforts. A cash box floated by trailing 100 franc notes; a swimmer grabbed as many as he could and stuffed them in his battledress pocket. The remains of big jellyfish killed by the explosions bobbed on the surface.

A Pay Corps private, wearing only his underpants and identity disc, was convinced that he saw a message from God in the sky. 'My Presence shall go with you,' the words from the Book of Exodus read. 'This was no hallucination on my part,' he wrote fifty-nine years later. 'I believe the words were intended for me.'

Morris Lashbrook was separated in the chaos from his friend 'Chippy' Moore as he drifted away from the *Lancastria*, clinging on to a lifeboat. He helped one badly wounded man, but he slipped away – Morris said he would never forget the look in his eyes as he died.

Stan Flowers, who had lost touch with his fellow Kent man, Wally Smith from the heavy transport unit, felt himself being dragged down by the water in the pockets of his battledress trousers. He asked another man to help him get them off. The man did so, and the trousers sank, carrying with them Stan's wallet in which he had kept the programme from a concert party and ten one franc notes. Soon afterwards, the other man was hit by a strafing bullet, and killed. Stan felt like giving up. Then, he remembered that it was his mother's birthday. That had the effect of pulling him round, with a fresh sense of survival.

Seeing some of his men in the water round him, Clem Stott shouted to them and stuck up a thumb. He spotted a destroyer which seemed nearby; but, when he started swimming towards it, he realised how far away it was.

A raft crowded with men singing 'Roll Out the Barrel' passed close, and Stott swam to it. But those on board shouted 'Get off! Get away!', and feet in grey army socks kicked him in the face. Drifting through the wreckage and burned and blackened bodies, he could not spot a living human being. He felt as if he was consigned to be among the dead, and then grew even more anxious as cramp seized his left leg.

In the crowd of survivors, a man shouted, 'Save me; I have a wife and three children' – he was pulled out of the water on to a raft. An upturned lifeboat was covered with men, most of them injured. Some could not hold on, and slipped away to sink below the surface. Clinging to a big wooden box, a young man from the Royal Artillery talked to the nine others round him of his home, his family and his fiancée. One by one, five of the others were overcome by exhaustion and let go. Then the young man cried out: 'My God, I have cramp', and dropped beneath the water.

Having abandoned his smart bicycle on the deck of the *Lancastria*, Sergeant George Youngs held on to an orange box with a group of men. Seven of them loosened their grip and sank.

Some ranted and raved. Others were silent, praying or thinking of their families. Two men, neither of whom could swim, pounded the water, silently locked in an embrace. They went under once, and surfaced with deathly faces. Silently, they disappeared once more, and were not seen again. A sapper clinging to an oar watched his best friend sink to his death unable to do anything to save him.

One man pushed his plank to another, saying, 'I can see your need is greater than mine.' An exhausted survivor lay half on a raft, his head down in the oil on the surface, raising it to cry out prayers. Another soldier told him to shut up and keep up his spirits, which would be a better path to salvation.

Two men floated together.

'Well, Charlie, when you are ready I am,' one said.

The other grasped a revolver attached round his neck by a string.

The first man shouted, 'Fire away.'

Two shots rang out as the man with the gun shot his companion and then himself.

CHAPTER 8

————

The Rescue

AS SOON AS THE *LANCASTRIA* began to list, a fleet of boats hurried out to rescue survivors. French fishing craft joined the destroyers, armed trawlers and tenders from the British flotilla. One rowing boat was manned by an elderly man and a boy. When the first warships arrived, a cry went up of 'The navy's here!' Among those they pulled from the water were the two Church Army sisters, Trott and Chamley, who had given their life belts to men in the sea. After three hours in the water, Alec Cuthbert and the man clinging to his life jacket were pulled on to a tiny boat with crab pots hanging along its side. In the hull, there were two corpses.

Michael Sheehan, from the *Lancastria*'s crew, saw a French tug sailing by, making no attempt to pick anybody up. At least one rowing boat set out from the shore on a scavenging mission. A British officer stood at the prow of a lifeboat levelling a revolver at people in the sea to keep them from climbing aboard and overloading the vessel. One swimmer reached up to catch the front of the boat. The officer shot him. Immediately afterwards, he, himself, toppled into the water – one account said he was shot by somebody inside the vessel, another that those on board pushed him into the sea. Men in the water began to pull themselves inside.

The skipper of a French boat, which picked up Morris Lashbrook and those in the lifeboat to which he had clung, said he was going to take them back to St-Nazaire. Crowded round the Frenchman, the rescued men insisted that he head out to sea, and transfer them to one of the ships in the British rescue fleet.

At first, each rescue boat did its own thing. But then they became better organised, forming a circle round the men in the water. One tug had a crane with a winch, and used it to lower men on hooks to pick up people and haul them aboard. Many of those pulled from the sea were naked, smothered in oil, burned or otherwise wounded. Sergeant Bertie Cook, who had been saved by the friend who hauled him on to a floating plank, wore nothing except his watch.

Reunited with his wife in the water, Clifford Tillyer gripped his 2-year-old daughter, Jacqueline, by her clothes with his teeth as they swam for safety. The RAF man, Peter Vinicombe, and the women on a table-like raft saw small boats approaching. The women started waving their arms and shouting 'Mon Dieu, Mon Dieu.' One of the rescue ships came alongside them, and took on the civilians. Vinicombe clung to a tyre on its side. Covered with black oil, he was transferred to a motor vessel, the *Cymbula*, where two Chinese crewmen washed him down. Only then did he discover that he had been hit in the arm by a tracer bullet.

The *Lancastria*'s electrician, Frank Brogden, watched the rescue ships, but they seemed unable to spot him in the mass of flotsam surrounding him. Thirty yards away, he saw a crew mate on a rescue boat. 'Keep your chin up,' the man shouted. 'We'll try to get to you.'

But as the rescue boats drew near him, they set up a wash that swept Brodgen further out into the estuary. 'That's it,' he thought.

Then a French tug sailed up, and its crew threw a hook over the side. Brogden scrambled aboard. He was covered in oil from head to toe; his white dungarees were completely black. It was 9 p.m.

The French sailors handed him a mug of hot, sweetened wine that made him vomit, doing himself a power of good by bringing up oil he had swallowed in his five hours in the sea.

Stan Flowers, who had been given fresh strength to survive by thinking of his mother's birthday, was pulled on to a long boat, and then put on a French tug where the crew gave him a sailor's jersey with an anchor embroidered on it. He was afraid that if he was taken back to St-Nazaire he would be captured by the Germans, so he was relieved when the destroyer, the *Havelock*, sailed by, and he was transferred. A big sailor who helped him on board handed him a mug of cocoa and a cigarette. Stan lay on the deck, looking back at the sea covered with bodies. Tied to the destroyer's rail were two dogs smeared with oil.

Soon, the decks of the rescue ships were as tightly packed as those of the *Lancastria* had been. Captain Fuller of the *John Holt* reckoned that 1100 people may have been brought on to his cargo ship.

When people pulled from the sea were found to be dead, the bodies were thrown back. 'We have only got room for the living,' a crewman said. On one French rescue boat, a doctor examined the black oily bodies covering the deck, and decided which were to be pitched into the sea. On another, a young woman whose legs had been broken died before she could be moved to a larger craft. On the *Havelock*, a very fat man sat propped up on a bench in a severe state of shock. Suddenly, he keeled over and died.

A man came up to Norman Driver to thank him for saving his life. He was upset that he had nothing he could give the sapper. Driver told him not to worry; they had both been saved. The man pressed something into the soldier's hand, saying, 'It's all I've got. Thank you.' It was a small packet with the picture of a lady on it – a French letter. Driver kept the condom for years.

Eleven-year-old Roger Legroux and his mother were pulled aboard a French fishing boat with Fernande Tips, whose mother was also picked up after three hours in the water. Roger and Madame Legroux were transferred to the *Havelock*. When they reached the destroyer, the unconscious boy was taken for dead, and his body was put on a pile of corpses on the deck.

His mother cried and screamed. Somebody gave Roger artificial respiration, and he came to. Soon afterwards, he was running round the boat with a Flemish boy of the same age.

Still, mother and son had a major concern – what had happened to Monsieur Legroux and his 13-year-old daughter from whom they had been separated as the *Lancastria* went down.

For the British troops, there was one familiar morale booster. Getting on board the *Havelock*, Sergeant Harry Pettit of the RASC relished 'endless supplies of hot, sweet tea, and how welcome it was'. On the French rescue boats, there was water, wine and cognac – one tug happened to have a large stock of condensed milk on board which the crew poured out for survivors. George Youngs of the RASC, who had abandoned his shiny bicycle on the *Lancastria*, gulped down water when he was hauled aboard a fishing boat. Then, he fell forward on his face from exhaustion.

A young man plucked from the sea sat with his head held as stiffly as if it was in a vice. The explosion of a bomb had driven a piece of wood into his neck just behind his ears. If he moved, he risked being killed. He died the following day on the way back to England, and was buried at sea.

Getting on to a French trawler, Sergeant Macpherson of the RAF headed for the engine room to try to dry out. Inside, covered by a blanket, sat a man who had been blinded by the bombing and fearfully lacerated by flying fragments. Boarding another French boat, John Edwards was met by great guffaws of laughter for his blue silk swimming trunks.

A Belgian woman, Julie Delfosse, was helped by Harry Pack, the soldier who had given up trying to get some beer when he had seen the crowd at the bar. Julie and Harry spent four hours together in the water before being picked up by a rowing boat – he was taken to a destroyer, while she was put on a French trawler where she was reunited with her son from whom she had been separated when the *Lancastria* went down.

Edwin Quittenton of the Royal Engineers managed to reach the side of the trawler as its gunner fired back at German plane attacks. He scrambled aboard, and threw ropes over the side to others. All around him on the ship, he recalled, were 'mutilated bodies, men badly burned, and amongst us, one woman and child. Out on the sea were hundreds of bodies, many past recognition, shot to pieces, machine-gunned or blown to pieces. At last came the order from the French captain that he could not take on any more men.'

A lifeboat filled with people came alongside the destroyer, the *Highlander*, among them an RAF man who had kept his shirt, collar and tie but nothing else. A sailor cut off his shirt with a jackknife, rubbed him down with cotton waste and gave him a duffel coat. Seeing the naked men covered with black oil, somebody on the destroyer began to sing Negro spirituals. At that, one of the officers recalled, 'we all felt better'.

One of the *Highlander*'s crew, Denis Maloney, looked over the side and saw the empty lifeboat bobbing up and down on the water. He jumped down into it, shouting 'Come on!' Two other young sailors followed. They took the oars while Maloney held the tiller, which he found very heavy. .

The boat reached a group of men in the water. One of those pulled on board the lifeboat was the Bren gunner, Fred Coe, who was given a towel to cover himself for modesty's sake. The survivors helped to rescue others. Soon, forty men were in the lifeboat. Five died there, all covered in oil. Their bodies were put back in the sea to make room for others.

Looking back, Maloney saw the *Highlander* sailing away, loaded to the gunwales with men. Round his lifeboat were screaming men and floating bodies while German planes swooped down, machine-gunning those in the water.

'War is war but that was murder,' Maloney said sixty years on. 'We were left stranded – on the *Highlander* they must have thought that they'd got hundreds on board and had lost three, so it was better to be off. We were all weak and it was getting dark.' Then a French motor-boat came by and threw a line to tow them to shore.

Maloney stayed in the boat until the rest had disembarked. One man was still on board – dead. Maloney walked over to the body, and took some letters from the pocket so that he could inform the family.

Clinging to the oar that had saved his life, Sergeant Major Picken made his way to a trawler. A rope was thrown down. He lost his grip, and went under. Still holding on to the oar, he rose to the surface and was hauled on board, unconscious. Coming to, he found himself in a small, dark cabin with other men. They broke open a cupboard which turned out to contain clothes. Picken donned a pair of pyjama trousers and a huge butcher's apron.

The man who had seen a message from God in the sky was picked up by a small boat soon afterwards, and put on HMS *Cambridgeshire*, which took on 800 men. German aircraft swooped on the vessel. A Lewis gun on board jammed, reducing her defensive capability. But the captain watched the planes, and twisted the wheel to avoid their bombs, which slid into the sea beside her, sending up plumes of water that soaked the men crowded on her decks.

Later, the captain put forward three of his men for gallantry awards. Ordinary Seaman Arthur Drage, he wrote, had saved some fifty men from drowning by taking charge of a lifeboat from the *Lancastria*. Coxswain Stanley Kingett had made 'repeated journeys in ship's boat to rescue exhausted men from water while under machine-gun fire from enemy planes'. Able Seaman William Reeves Perrin had kept up 'continuous machine-gun fire, in an attempt to prevent enemy planes machine-gunning men in water. Probably brought down one plane, but this cannot be confirmed.'[1]

Sidney Dunmall, whose premonition had sent him up from the queue for chocolate bars at the Purser's office as the bombs were about to fall, survived by moving from a plank to an inflated rubber raft. The six men on it weighed it down almost to the level of the sea, but they improvised paddles out of pieces of boxwood and reached the *Cambridgeshire*. Dunmall was too weak to climb the scaling net on the side of the ship, so the others grabbed hold of him and pulled him up on to the deck where he lay by a drum filled with depth charges. After a time, he went down to the boiler room and sat in front of the open furnaces to dry off and get warm. A naked man asked if he could spare any clothes. Dunmall handed over his shirt.

On the *Highlander*, half a dozen men who had been taken for dead when they were pulled from the water were brought round by artificial respiration. After three hours in the sea, the Tillyers and their daughter, Jacqueline, were brought on board. The destroyer's steward, 'Ding Dong' Bell from Dover, took the 2-year-old girl to the captain's cabin to revive her by dipping her into alternate basins of hot and cold water. Then he rubbed the oil off her body, clothed her in a naval sweater, washed her hair, arranged it with the captain's brush and comb, and carried her up to the deck wrapped in a blanket. After that he sold a bottle of whisky to one of the survivors who gave some to a naked man who came into the wardroom, and who turned out to be a lieutenant colonel.

Several rescue boats tried to pick up a Geordie who was so covered with oil that it was impossible to catch hold of him. Eventually, a sailor snared him with a boathook that cut through his underpants into the flesh below. Before leaving Newcastle, he had gone shopping with his wife for a pair of pants. One pair in the shop cost half-a-crown, another only 1s. 11½*d*. He had bought the cheaper ones: now he wished he had taken the more expensive pair, reckoning that they would have been stronger. But he was saved, at the cost of a big gash in his buttocks.

At the front of a small boat lowered by the destroyer, the *Havelock*, stood a giant sailor, completely naked. He scooped men out of the sea, slung them over his shoulder and took them to the back of the craft. The other sailor steering the boat called the huge man 'Pricky', and one of those he saved said he appeared to be 'very aptly named'.

The *Cymbula* took on a stream of survivors from smaller boats, including one soldier clutching a small dog which the ship's mainly Chinese crew held on to and called 'Fifi'. The Second Radio Officer, Richard Wilkins, handed a Penguin book of English poetry to one soldier, and a vest to another who was naked. Wilkins tried to give artificial respiration to a soldier who had swallowed a lot of water and oil by pressing down on his back with both hands, but had to stop because the man was in such pain.

Percy Fairfax of the RASC floated for four hours on an inflated cushion with a rope trailing from a raft looped round his shoulder. Then he saw a rowing boat coming towards him. Two French sailors on board were using the oars to move kitbags floating on the sea. The men on the raft cried for help. But the Frenchmen were scavengers, and pushed away those in the water.

A strong swimmer grabbed Fairfax's shoulder, breaking the

loop of rope. Percy gave him a dig in the ribs with his elbow, and, resting on his cushion, managed to reach the raft. When he tried to climb on board, it threatened to sink with his weight. Two men threw him off. He made another attempt. The men held his head under the water for a time. Then one grabbed him by the collar and dragged him to grasp a ring. Fairfax asked the man for his name. 'There are no heroes or names on this raft,' he replied. 'We are all pals, so stick together and all keep quiet.'

A steamer passed by, and those on the raft called for help. But it did not stop, though its wash turned them round and carried them into clean water. Finally, a French ship stopped to pick them up.

For the first time, Fairfax let go of his cushion to grasp a rope thrown down to him. But his hands were so coated with oil that it slipped through his fingers like an eel. He went under. Rising to the surface again, he grasped another rope, which he put round his waist. The knot slipped, and he went down again.

Rising to the surface, Fairfax tried to grab the plaited rope on the side of the French boat. He could not get a grip. Down came another rope. Exhausted and knowing he could not last much longer, Percy took it in his hands, arms and teeth, wrapped it round his body and twice round his right arm, binding the end with his left hand. That was enough to get him hoisted up to the deck, where he passed out.

Coming round, he found he was lying with his head in the lap of a woman rescuer. He got up and walked to the covered-in part of the deck where men sat silently, drenched in oil. After a while, he asked an officer for the time. It was nine at night – five hours after the *Lancastria* had gone down.

*

The woman in whose lap Percy Fairfax had come round was Joan Rodes, the Englishwoman whose French husband was away at the front and who had organised hospital services in La Baule. She had been offered a place on an evacuation ship, but she decided to stay in France.

Though she was heavily pregnant, Rodes joined a friend of hers, Michel Luciani, to sail into the bay of St-Nazaire in his fishing smack, dodging mines dropped by German planes. Helped by a prominent local businessman, Pierre Huni, and a Briton living in the area, Henry Boyd, they ferried nineteen badly injured men back to La Baule, where food and drink were laid on. In the Hermitage, the luxury hotel that had been turned into a hospital, Joan prepared beds for the wounded. But they were so badly hurt that it was decided to take them by road to St Joseph's hospital in St-Nazaire for treatment.

Huni and Rodes set off again with Luciani in his boat, the *Saint Michel,* to undertake more rescue work. It was a nightmare journey. On the way, they were strafed. Joan Rodes flung herself on the deck, her face white from the pain of her pregnancy. Among survivors of the *Lancastria,* she became known as 'the Angel of St-Nazaire'.

Huni, a French delegate to the International Red Cross, used his limousine to ferry survivors who had come ashore. He tried to set up a final evacuation for some of the remaining British troops on a French boat, but the captain refused to take them – anyway the ship was waterlogged.

Getting back to La Baule, Joan Rodes helped to arrange for the burial of bodies from the *Lancastria* washed up on the wide beach of the resort. A local woman donated a field for the purpose. Broken wine bottles were put at the head of the graves with the men's identity tags and other personal belongings under the glass. Later the owner of the field put up white crosses, and cultivated flowers round the graves.

In the following days, a French general and a British destroyer captain both advised Rodes to leave France. Again, she decided to stay to do what she could to help British soldiers to escape. When a party of German officers turned up to take over her hospital, she put up a sign reading 'Contagious', telling them she was treating patients suffering from typhus. After the Germans left hurriedly, Rodes recruited a young priest and nuns to remove valuable X-ray equipment to prevent it falling into enemy hands.

Led by a young officer with a monocle, the Germans came back to have the hospital disinfected. As this was being done, Rodes saw the officer mistreating an elderly woman, and upbraided him.

'You should lower your eyes, and hang your head in shame,' he shouted, 'for you forget you were beaten.'[2]

'Beaten! I am not beaten! I am British!' Rodes replied, walking off to the dispensary.

The officer followed her. She told him that her husband was at the front, and that her father-in-law was a general who had lost one eye and one arm in battle.

'You are not afraid?' the German asked.

'That is not a word in my vocabulary,' she responded.

'Oh well, the war will soon be ended, and it's only a matter of time before we invade and conquer England.'

'Not on your life,' Rodes said. 'No German will ever set foot on English soil unless as a prisoner.'

The officer said he saluted her as one soldier to another.

A few days later, Rodes had a miscarriage. She remained in bed for two years suffering from fever and thrombosis and was then a semi-invalid. Still, she operated a secret radio for the Resistance, and hid British servicemen in the cellars of her family-in-law's house until they could find an escape route out of France.

Pierre Huni became a member of the Resistance: in December 1941, he was questioned by the Gestapo who raided the YMCA in Paris while he was visiting it. He was released after two-and-a-half hours. The captain of the fishing smack, Michel Luciani, went on to sabotage German patrol boats on the western coast of France. Their British partner, Henry Boyd, was arrested and died while interned at the American hospital in Paris.

A 15-year-old French boy, Gaston Noblanc, watched as the German planes swooped on the estuary and the port. He had got to know the British troops while working as a newspaper delivery boy, taking copies of the *Daily Mail* and *Daily Express* to camps round St-Nazaire. Now, he joined a relative on a tug that went out to try to save men from the sea, lowering a small boat to pull them from the water. 'It was Hell,' he recalled, 'abominable, the height of horror.'

Like Rodes and Huni, Gaston Noblanc joined the Resistance. He used his newspaper delivery round to gather information on German military installations, passing it to London through an underground network run by the Mayor of La Baule. He spotted U-boats using the pens at St-Nazaire and informed the British through a clandestine radio. Captured by the Gestapo, he was tortured, and badly burned.

*

Captain Sharp was floating, exhausted, in the sea when the *Lancastria*'s surgeon, Dr Shaw, spotted him and went to help; they were rescued after four hours in the water. Two men from their ship on a rescue boat saw them. 'Holy smoke,' one called to the other, 'there's the Captain.'

Sharp was pulled on board with some difficulty given his heavy frame and the slippery oil on his clothes. He was taken to the *Havelock*, and then transferred with hundreds of others to the damaged liner, the *Oronsay*, where the first bombing had stopped all the clocks at 1.15. As men crossed a plank between the destroyer and the passenger ship, the rolling sea made some tumble into the water.

Already on the *Oronsay*, Harry Grattidge gave Sharp a drink from a brandy flask he had in his pocket. Then the Chief Officer changed his water-sodden Cunard Line uniform with its gold braid for a corporal's jacket which he put on over his woollen underwear. The liner's main salon was turned into a sick bay: some of the men were, Grattidge recalled, 'so burned you could hardly credit that a life survived beneath the raw and weeping tissue'.[3]

A French tug pulled alongside with 500 men, who crossed to the liner except for a Belgian who refused to board the British ship and was taken back to St-Nazaire. The men were given blankets which they wrapped round their bodies and heads. Coming to in the semi-darkness after passing out when he was pulled from the sea, Percy Braxton of the RAF thought he was surrounded by a crowd of hooded monks. Others put on torn-up sacks. Some of the injured had to be carried on to the deck, and lay there smoking cigarettes. For a few, it was their last smoke. When they died, they were sewn into hammocks and buried at sea.

A Salvation Army man and his wife, who had travelled from

Paris to St-Nazaire to join the evacuation with nothing more than the clothes they wore and a cache of francs, put up money to buy the survivors cigarettes and drinks; they explained to Grattidge that, though their organisation did not normally encourage use of stimulants, this was a special situation.

Going down to the sick bay cabin on the *Oronsay*, Grattidge saw a familiar figure, tending to survivors in his shirt sleeves: Lieutenant Colonel Earle, whom he had met on the liner, *Carpathia*, twenty-six years before.

When the Chief Officer hailed him, the other man raised his eyebrows and nodded. He might have been interrupted reading *The Times* in his club. Grattidge introduced himself, but Earle did not remember him. After the Chief Officer gave some more information about himself, the surgeon said: 'Oh, really, glad you were picked up. A good show.' Then he went back to his work. It was, Grattidge reflected in his memoirs, a marvel of British imperturbability – 'while there were men like Lt-Col. Earle, I thought, there always indeed would be an England.'[4]

What he did not mention was that Earle was operating without anaesthetics.

Wing Commander Macfadyen and Captain Griggs also ended up on the *Oronsay* after being picked up by overloaded French rescue ships. Seeing men without life jackets arriving, the Captain insisted that they should go. 'It wasn't being heroic,' he remembered. 'I was too breathless to climb up a ship's ladder just then.'

On board, Griggs reached into his jacket pocket and found a packet of twenty Players cigarettes still in its cellophane. The packet was, miraculously, nearly bone dry. He lit one himself and handed round the other nineteen.

The Captain was handed a shirt, shorts and gym shoes. He went in search of a bathroom. A steward offered him a hip bath full of hot fresh water which, unlike salt water, would remove the oil.

It was only then that the reaction to the event set in as Griggs suddenly realised how easily he could have been among the dead. 'The thought had not struck me before,' he recalled. 'I had felt no fear on the ship or in the water, only anger.'

Sitting on the deck, he watched a naked man black with oil from head to foot dive off the side of the ship and swim out to bring survivors back. He saved five men before exhaustion stopped him. Later, Griggs made a point of finding out who he was and reporting his exploit to the War Office, which awarded him the Military Cross.

The Welsh accountant, Captain Clement Stott, saw a fishing boat close to him. His head felt 'like a forty shilling pot' as they said in his part of the country. But it was his last chance of surviving, and he got within reach of one of the tyres hanging from the side of the ship.

When he stretched out his arm to grab it, his hand slid off, and he swallowed a mouthful of oily water. Then, Stott recalled, 'a line suddenly came whizzing through the air, my hand caught it; but again I had no grip. I was covered in oil to the last square inch and by now my strength was almost gone. I just floated, unable to move any of my limbs.'

The swell lifted him away from the boat. The dirty old car tyre on its side seemed a symbol of life. A man on board put his hands to his mouth, and shouted '*Courage mon vieux!*'

Stott thrust out his left arm. It hit something. He turned to see what it was. A dead body.

That seemed the end. For the only time in his life, he said to himself, 'I've had it!' Then, suddenly, he thought of his wife and children. 'At that terrible moment,' he recalled, 'my mind was all at once filled with a life-like picture of them all. It gave me another ounce of strength and a new determination.

'"I will not die." The words formed in me. I had been a lucky and happy man in my home life, no family sorrow had ever got my dear wife or me down, and I damn well wanted to see them all again – this side of heaven! I would see them again!

'I braced myself and gritted my teeth and made ready for my last attempt. Three seconds I'd give myself. I counted "One! Two!"'

A big swell flung him on to the fishing boat where he passed out as it took him to St-Nazaire. There, a medical orderly insisted on giving him a new officer's jacket, covered with blood. Stott was moved to a troop ship, and provided with hot soapy water, but it would not wash off the oil. He was also handed a mug of cocoa which he could hardly keep down. Finally, he was given a big coat. He pictured himself at that moment – 'A little, middle-aged man in pince-nez and an officer's overcoat . . . which might have fitted Jack Dempsey.'

CHAPTER 9

———

St-Nazaire

AT 10 P.M., THE PORT COMMAND in St-Nazaire got round to reporting the sinking of the *Lancastria* to French naval headquarters. Marked 'Secret', the message limited itself to noting: 'British liner *Lancastria* carrying evacuated troops hit by German bomb and sank on the Grand Charpentier roads at 1516gmt.' There was no further entry in French naval records.

The men who were not taken straight to one of the rescue ships in the estuary were landed on the quayside at St-Nazaire. It was night by now, and there were no lights because of intermittent German air raids.

The wharf was crowded with survivors. 'Some was injured,' the electrician, Frank Brogden, recalled. 'Some was in a state of shock. Some was clothed. Some wasn't clothed at all, all black from head to toe with oil fuel.'

Frenchwomen dug holes in bales of straw on the dockside, and helped men climb inside for shelter. An old lady put a white apron round one soldier, who had lost most of his clothes. A Red Cross unit tended to the wounded as best it could.

Two Royal Navy officers approached a group of men lying on the straw covered with blankets. They offered a choice – either to stay and be taken to hospital, risking capture by the Germans, or to board one of the freighters still in the harbour. Most chose to go, and spent the night on the ships, which were the targets of unsuccessful bombing, before heading for the open sea at dawn.

Fleets of ambulances drove those who could not leave, or did not want to do so, to the town's convent hospital. Nursing nuns met them. The first job was to clean the oil from the soldiers' bodies.

Sergeant Miller of the Buffs, who had passed out after being picked up by a fishing boat, came round when nuns threw buckets of hot water over him. As the nurses scrubbed Private Proctor of the RASC, he vomited up oil and was given an injection that made him sleep till the next morning.

Sergeant Youngs of the RASC was driven by ambulance to a ward that was spotlessly white except for black marks on the walls from the soldiers' hands. He was put in a children's area where a boy was coming round from an appendix operation. One of the staff removed his filthy clothes, and he was taken to a bathroom where he was 'acutely aware' that it was a nun who scrubbed his body. After which, a doctor gave him a sleeping injection.

In another religious hospital, there was little soap or hot water, and the nuns handed the men sheets with which to wipe themselves as clean as they could. Then they wrapped them in blankets and took them to lie on palliasses between the beds, telling the men to be quiet so as not to disturb the patients. Local people brought clothes – Frank Brodgen was given a pair of velveteen trousers and a shirt; he looped strips of old carpet round his feet as slippers. The oil had not been scrubbed off, however. 'What the patients thought in the morning when they woke up and saw a bunch of nigger minstrels between the beds!' Brodgen wrote later.

In one large hall, men were given coffee or tea, laced with brandy, rum or whisky. There were twenty bathtubs of hot water, with two or three men using each.

'It was a case of first one leg in the bath, then the other, then the arms and the head,' Bill Slater, of the Pay Corps, recalled. 'Then the back. Each man had to take turns in washing the back of the other. He cleaned mine and then I cleaned his. When there was more diesel oil in the bath than water, or when the water was too cold, two ladies took it away and came back with more.'

With much of the oil removed, the men dressed from a pile of old clothes. Slater picked up a vest, and a pair of trousers which had belonged to a man whose stomach was five inches bigger than his but whose legs were five inches shorter. He also got a blanket, but no shoes or socks. Then he and others who had been cleaned up were driven back to the dock in an ambulance. On the way, Slater was violently sick from the mixture of coffee, brandy, rum and diesel oil which he had swallowed. 'I felt terrible, but it was all for the best,' he added. 'It helped to clear the stomach.'

When Denise Petit of the Banque de France arrived at her home that night, she saw a van stopping in the street outside.

Men got out. Were they really men, she wondered. They were filthy, naked and shivering. Some were wrapped in blankets. Having unloaded them, the van driver headed back for the docks.

There had been an ambulance post beside her house, but it had been moved, and there was nobody to look after the men. So Denise called her mother and neighbours and passers-by. They took the men inside their homes, washed them, and gave them clean clothes and hot alcohol. A British lieutenant called the roll.

Denise could see that the men were suffering all over their bodies, and in their eyes and noses where the oil had penetrated. They found it difficult to breathe, but none complained. As soon as they were ready, those who could went back to the docks to re-embark, having heard rumours that the Germans were already in Nantes. Denise and her mother nursed others through the night as German planes swirled overhead.

Joe Sweeney was brought ashore after being picked up by a lifeboat and put on a French trawler. He was naked, having taken off all his clothes to enable him to swim more easily.

Walking carefully because of his bare feet, he crossed the road at the docks and went into a bar filled with raucous soldiers. All he wanted was peace and quiet. Noticing a hatch door below the bar, he scrambled through it into a dark back room. The *patronne* strode in, not realising in the darkness that the French-speaking Sweeney was naked. He told her what had happened to him on the *Lancastria*.

'Wait here,' she shouted. A minute later, she returned with a half-full bottle of brandy, a packet of Gauloises and a box of matches. As her eyes became accustomed to the darkness, she saw he had no clothes on.

'Go on! Get out! Now,' she said, showing him through the back door, and then adding in a whisper, '*Bonne chance, gamin.*'

Thanking her, Sweeney went out into the night. He crossed the road to sit on the pavement, sipping the brandy. It made him feel warmer. Euphoria overcame him as he smoked one cigarette after another, and fantasised about escaping to Spain.

When a teenage girl walked by, Sweeney got up to greet her. She asked if he was hurt.

'No, I'm all right; just frozen stiff,' he replied. They sat down and she asked him about the *Lancastria*. Suddenly a flare lit up overhead and she saw that he was naked.

'Good Lord! You've got no clothes on,' she cried, jumping up.

Then she added, '*Pauvre homme!*' and told him to wait.

A few minutes later, she returned with a pair of her brother's riding breeches and a flannel shirt. The breeches were too small – Joe had to rip the seams to get them on. The shirt was too small, too, so he and the girl tore the neck and sleeves. She also produced a little bottle of cognac, more cigarettes and matches. They chatted some more. Then she left saying, '*Au revoir et bonne chance.*'

Sweeney sat down again on the pavement feeling elated. An ambulance picked him up. Inside, he passed his bottles round to the other passengers. They were dropped by a coal ship on which they sailed from St-Nazaire. The boat was so crowded that Joe slept standing up.

*

An English-speaking nun in a convent hospital warned a sergeant from the Buffs of rumours – false as it turned out – that the Germans were on the outskirts of the town. Clad in only a blanket, the soldier made his way to the quay where he found a uniform abandoned by an officer. Wearing the jacket and trousers of a lieutenant colonel, he got on board the cargo ship, *John Holt.* He was one of the more fortunate ones on the cargo boat. The ship's captain sent a signal to Britain that he was 'returning with 829 survivors from *Lancastria,* many without clothing'.

Signalman Leonard Forde, who had driven his wireless truck across France and then failed to get on a tender taking men out to the *Lancastria,* was stuck on the quay till after night fell. Losing patience, he and a couple of dozen men waded out to a rowing boat floating off the docks, and steered it to one of the remaining rescue ships. He was too tired to ask what its name was.

British troops were still arriving in St-Nazaire to join the final exodus from France. Orders were to get out as many men as possible, and the British were clearly in no state to withstand the Germans if they reached the far west. Still, Major Fred Hahn thought he should do all he could to get valuable equipment home. So he put together a seventy-eight-vehicle convoy from Nantes with materiel from a workshop. When it reached the airfield outside St-Nazaire, he was told that no more vehicles were being allowed into the town. Everything was to be dumped at the airfield and set alight. All that mattered was to save as many men as possible, and to leave nothing for the enemy.

Refusing to accept this, Hahn and a colonel accompanying

him instructed the convoy to head south with a guard of twenty infantrymen. They hoped it might reach Bordeaux, where there could be sea transport back to Britain for the equipment which included secret radar parts. Having seen the convoy off, Hahn and the colonel went back with some of their men to liaise with the last remaining British staff at their headquarters in Château Douet Garnier outside Nantes.

There, they breakfasted in the basement of a large house with a major who had been in charge of the first line of British defence of Nantes. Half a dozen French people were also in the room, including two French women, whom Hahn described as 'youngish' and 'both very much in negligé.'[1]

It was a very hot day and the lady on Hahn's right was 'wearing only a diaphanous pale blue nightie which did little to conceal her superb figure'. Sitting pressed hard up against her, even in the dim light of the basement, Hahn could not help noticing how the silky sheen 'moulded and embellished her perfectly formed breasts'. Under different circumstances, he acknowledged, he might have been 'very interested in her. She was about 30 years old and in perfect shape.' But he had not slept for two days or eaten for more than twelve hours, and had urgent business to attend to. So he concentrated on military matters.

The major had a plan of the British line of defence in the sector, but he said his men had already left for St-Nazaire, and he was going to follow them after breakfast. Finishing his meal, Hahn went to the British General Headquarters where he found a general and his aide-de-camp.

'Where do you keep your whisky?' Hahn asked.

'Plenty in the cupboard,' the ADC replied. 'Help yourself.'

Next, Hahn went back to Douet Garnier for a battle conference. Another participant, Colonel Shorthouse, of the South

Staffordshire Regiment, wanted to try to hold the Germans on the road from Le Mans to give more time for the evacuation from St-Nazaire. But he only had two tanks, which had been damaged and then repaired. Hahn lent him twenty of his men who set out on the road with the two tanks – 'the last rearguard in France,' as Hahn wrote later.[2] However, the tanks broke down, and they did not meet any Germans.

Hahn and a colonel called Suggate, set off in a Humber Snipe staff car to catch up with the convoy they had sent towards Bordeaux. Before long, they came across one truck blazing by the roadside. Then they found the other lorries also on fire. The packing cases loaded on to them had been smashed open. Petrol had been poured over the contents.

There was no sign of any soldiers. A dispatch rider had ridden up to the convoy with an order from the embarkation officer in St-Nazaire for them to destroy the trucks and equipment, and get to the ships. Hahn's driver looked at the flaming vehicles and said, 'The bastards!'

They drove to St-Nazaire. When they reached the perimeter of the airfield outside the town, an officer told them to ditch their car in a field, and to burst open the petrol tank. Hahn said they planned to return to Nantes, so they would keep the vehicle. In the distance they heard the sound of bombing. Somebody told them a ship had been hit. Hahn reckoned that the bombs did not sound very heavy, and would not do much damage to a big boat.

Despite the instructions not to do so, they drove on towards St-Nazaire. But the jam of men on the road was so great that they left the Humber, and walked. As they got into the town, Hahn heard a cry of 'Freddie' from a grimy, oil-bespattered man coming up a flight of steps. It was a soldier he knew, Major Leslie Bradbury, who had been on the

Lancastria and had got back ashore. Bradbury said he had 400 of his men with him but 'the Frenchies won't let us have any grub. They say they have not enough for themselves.'

Hahn offered to drive back to Nantes to get food. First, he and Colonel Suggate went into a café where French people were breakfasting on rolls and coffee.

'For us, the war is ended,' a man at the bar said as the Englishmen came in. 'Soon Hitler will conquer England.'

Hahn replied that the British were leaving now, but would be back. He bought rolls and coffee and took them to a table.

The man at the bar called him back, and offered Hahn and Suggate cognacs.

The two British officers drove back to Nantes, and made sure no men had been left behind there. They had a good dinner at La Coupole restaurant. After which, they motored in the Humber to St-Nazaire through a clear night under a bright moon.

CHAPTER 10

———

The Way Back

THE FIRST MENTION of the disaster in the British Naval War Diary for 17 June came in a single succinct sentence which stated that, 'The number of casualties is not yet known.'[1] A second entry added optimistically that 3733 of 5500 on board had been rescued. A third reported: 'Had on board 5200 troops and a number of women and children, about 2500 saved out of total of about 5500. 70 of crew of 330 lost.'

Another entry for the same day recorded a signal sent to Alan Brooke as he weighed up his plans. 'French Army has been ordered to cease fighting.' A bracketed addition read: '(Note it is thought this statement correct.)' Then somebody wrote 'in' in ink in front of 'correct'. Given Pétain's broadcast twenty-four hours earlier, the navy seemed to be living in a dream world.

*

Reaching St-Nazaire, Brooke's driver parked their car in a lane that offered concealment from the German planes. A man was sent to find the destroyer aboard which the British commander would leave France for the second time in less than three weeks. He returned with news of the sinking of the *Lancastria*. No destroyers were available, he added. All were needed to rescue survivors.

Brooke had a choice of boarding the armoured trawler, the *Cambridgeshire*, which was leaving that night, or staying to wait for a bigger boat the next day. He picked the first, hoping it was sufficiently small and insignificant not to attract the attention of the German pilots. It had no rafts or life belts, having used them all to save 800 to 900 men from the *Lancastria*.

The number of survivors on the adapted trawler would have made her unseaworthy once she got out into the Atlantic. So she landed the seriously wounded at St-Nazaire, and transferred some others to the fruit ship, the *John Holt*. The cargo boat headed down the estuary, through a minefield and, its captain signalled, 'going fast for home'.

Sidney Dunmall, the private from the Pay Corps, was among those transferred. He was told to go into a hold where he lay on a duck board in the dim light. There was not much conversation. One of the other men was wearing only a great coat with the stripes of a wing commander.

Every part of the *John Holt* was packed with men. The smoke room had been turned into a hospital, with two men in each bed. Others lay up on the deck. Curtains, tablecloths, bedding were used as clothing. Though it was a warm June night, the heating system was kept on to give comforting heat.

The Chief Steward went up to the bridge to ask the captain what to do to nourish the survivors. Soup was distributed – it was watery, but 'tasted lovely', Morris Lashbrook recalled. One survivor got his in the lid of a tobacco tin. Sidney Dunmall was handed rice, a dry biscuit, and a mug of water. There was also plenty of rum on board – kept for the loaders at African fruit ports when they worked overtime. So the captain told the steward to make buckets of tea, and pour a bottle into each.

Alan Brooke found the *Cambridgeshire* covered in sticky oil, 'an indescribable mess . . . with discarded clothes lying all over the place'. It had soaked into the carpets; and the white walls of the passageways and cabins were, he wrote, 'covered with impressions of every part of the human anatomy'.[2] The smell permeated the boat. The General went to work cleaning his cabin, which had previously been occupied by survivors pulled out of the sea. After half an hour, he gave up, and went to lie on deck. Around him, three air raids hit the port during the night.

The *Cambridgeshire* pulled out along the estuary at 3 a.m., passing the huge tomb of the *Lancastria* lying on the sea bed. As it headed to the high seas, the captain received a signal asking him to provide protection for a group of boats leaving St-Nazaire. He conferred with Brooke, and they agreed to form a convoy to sail round the Brittany peninsula.

Lying under the stars, Brooke thanked God that he and the remains of the BEF had escaped. Suddenly, a young sailor ran round the deck, screaming, 'Can't you see they are all drowning? Why are you not doing anything? Oh, God, we must do something for them.' He was held, and fed a drink of aspirins ground into milk. Calming down, he slept for a couple of hours; but when he awoke he began raving again, and had to be given more of the liquid.

When day broke, Brooke posed for a photograph with his staff, the ship's captain and a French officer. Despite his night on the deck, the General looked as trim as ever. In front of him sat a sailor in a singlet. 'It is an extraordinary contrast to find oneself sailing along on a lovely day surrounded by a calm sea, with no refugees, no columns of troops, no problems and no decisions to make,' he noted in his diary. 'A wonderful enforced rest'.[3]

When the sea became choppy in the afternoon, some of the soldiers on the *Cambridgeshire* could not keep their food down. But Brooke had no difficulty digesting his high tea of sardines and buttered toast.

Back in St-Nazaire, injured British soldiers and airmen were rushed from their beds to a shelter when air raids came near the hospitals. Then they were brought clothes, and taken to the dock where they found a hostile group of local inhabitants. A French cargo boat tied up on the quay refused to take on any of them.

A message to London from Brooke that night had warned: 'Ordinary Frenchmen believe that we evacuated Dunkirk without consulting French and are now doing the same.' Anti-British feeling was animated by the defeatists who had taken over the government, their local sympathisers and the belief that their ally had lived down to the German warnings that it would prove untrustworthy in the last resort. For most French, the priority now was to end the fighting.

But anti-British feeling was by no means universal, and was tempered by help and friendship from some. Civilians sent the wounded clothes, and applauded one group as it was moved from a religious to a military hospital.

A nurse warned a Sherwood Foresters in her hospital that the Germans were coming. He wrapped a blanket round himself, and left, carrying his wallet, money and army pay book. Joining three other men he met in the town, he took a ferry across the river, and hitched a lift in a lorry driven by a young Frenchman, who took them south as far as Bordeaux, where the British consul helped them find passage home.

After seeing the *Lancastria* hit in the bay, Vic Flowers, whose premonition had kept him off the liner, climbed down from the cliffs overlooking the estuary with the two other RAF men who had joined him in turning back from the tender. They walked to the road to Nantes, and hailed an army lorry heading for Brest. There, they boarded an evacuation liner, the *Strathaird*. On board, Flowers was given a kipper sandwich and a mug of hot, very sweet tea.

Also heading towards Brest, the Duggan family and the other two carloads of British civilians from Nantes had found a fan belt and repaired their broken-down vehicle. Reaching the coast, the convoy was stopped by French troops at a bridge, which they were planning to blow up. The soldiers were clearly very jittery, and it took some discussion before one shouted '*Allez vite!*' and waved them across. The bridge was never destroyed.

Eddie Duggan drove to the docks in Brest and negotiated with the crew of an evacuation ship to be allowed on board.

In all, thirty civilians were waiting to be taken off – Madame de Gaulle is thought to have been among them. Eventually, they were given permission, and went up the gangplank, young John Duggan cradling his Bedlington terrier in his arms.

As they climbed on to the ship, two big dogs started fighting on the deck. A sailor shouted that no dogs would be allowed on board. Eddie Duggan grabbed the terrier from John's arms, ran down the gangplank and handed it to a sentry. 'Find a home for it, or shoot it,' he called.

His son was devastated. He could hear the dog barking for him. Sitting on a bunk of the family's cabin, he began to sob. Then the door opened. An RAF sergeant came in, and unbuttoned his uniform jacket. Inside was the terrier – the sergeant had jumped down from the ship on to the quayside, taken the dog, stuffed it inside his jacket and come back on board with it.

The captain of the *Highlander* took a loudhailer and announced to the survivors on the deck: 'We've got no radio, no food, no escort, and we are listing ten degrees to port. Where are we going?'

'Back to Blighty!' came the reply.

On the destroyer, the *Havelock*, the dead were laid out in lifeboats in piles like stacks of corn. One man was found to be still alive. At 10.30 at night, the captain said he was ready to move off, and that the corpses would be left in the sea. A volley was to be fired in their honour, but then it was realised that this might set off panic among survivors still in a state of shock. So the dead were buried at sea with no last salute.

Moving more slowly than usual because of her fouled propeller, the *Havelock* was heavily overcrowded as she headed for home. In the night, she suffered engine failure. During the repairs, heavy gear was dropped, making a loud noise that the edgy passengers took for a torpedo bursting.

Among those on board was a civilian passenger from the *Lancastria* called Green, who had been picked up with his young daughter by a French tug and transferred to the warship. An officer on the destroyer refused to believe that Claudine was Green's daughter because she was speaking French.

'You take the child and see what her reactions are,' Green said.

The naval officer took hold of the girl who immediately started to scream and held out her arms to Green crying, 'Daddy, daddy, daddy.'

Papers drawn up fifty-six years later for the obituary of the *Havelock*'s captain, Barry Stevens, who had transferred to the *Highlander* after his own ship's propeller accident, contain an intriguing reference to the destroyer having carried 'a large quantity of French government gold'.[4] There is no other mention of this elsewhere, and French sources record their country's gold having been taken to Africa or the United States. It is possible that the gold in question may have been that stored by the British forces in the Banque de France in St-Nazaire. But Stevens was subsequently made a Commander of the Légion d'Honneur – according to the notes, drawn up by an admiral, for the rescue of French gold.

*

In all, 23,000 men left St-Nazaire in the night of 17–18 June. The biggest ship in the flotilla steaming back to England was the damaged liner, the *Oronsay*, with thousands on board, some of whom had swarmed up nets hung over the side. The direct hit on the *Oronsay*'s bridge by a German bomb at lunchtime had destroyed the chart, steering and wireless rooms, as well as breaking her captain's leg. Holed, she was taking in water which was being extracted by the auxiliary pumps.

The captain had been told he could land the men back in St-Nazaire, but he chose to head for home, leaving at dusk. A young officer addressed the men on the deck, warning them that England was hundreds of miles away, that there was no escort, a 10-degree list to port, no food and no bridge.

Using the auxiliary steering gear, the captain sailed by a pocket compass, the sextant and a sketch map of France. Since the bomb had destroyed the wireless, a call was put out for somebody who knew semaphore to act as a signaller when she came towards the coast of England, where she picked up an escort of the heavy cruiser HMS *Shropshire* and a Sunderland flying boat. A soldier volunteered, but admitted that his skill was only of Boy Scout standard. He was stood down when an army signaller was found. As she pulled in to Plymouth, the *Oronsay* was listing so acutely that she could not berth, and the men had to be ferried ashore on small boats.

One of the smaller boats in the flotilla heading towards England was the pleasure yacht formerly owned by the Wills tobacco company, which had become HMS *Oracle*. She sailed without a pilot, her crew throwing down a plumb line to chart a course. At one point, they picked up a submarine sounding, and dropped depth charges, but they got back to Plymouth without any trouble. Among those on board was a small group of soldiers and the *Lancastria* electrician, Frank Brogden, along with the crew from another ship, the *Teresias*, who had rowed to safety after their vessel was sunk by bombing as she entered the estuary the previous day.

Major Fred Hahn and Colonel Suggate were late leavers after their final drive to and from Nantes. When they got to the quay they found it still packed with long lines of men. Though he considered them 'fine chaps', Hahn described them as 'untrained and undisciplined'.[5] Equipment had been dumped helter-skelter. When a flight of four German planes passed low overhead, the men watched them apathetically, making no attempt to get under cover. Instead of diving and spraying the soldiers with machine-gun fire, the aircraft flew on their way.

Hahn and Colonel Suggate were taken out to the 10,000-ton freighter, the *City of Mobile*, which was full of men. The eighteen cabin berths were reserved for nurses; armed guards were posted at the doors to make sure they were not molested. There was no food. There should have been half a pint of water per person, but soldiers had run off all the drinking water so there was none. The dining salon was crammed: some slept on the tables, some on ladders, their limbs wrapped round the rungs. Hahn noticed that some of the men pilfered the belongings of others.

The *City of Mobile* joined a convoy of six vessels, including a tramp steamer that had been torpedoed in the bow and had what Hahn called 'a hole a double decker bus could have driven through'. Passage out of the estuary was delayed because the Germans had dropped parachute mines. After a

Sunderland flying boat detonated them, the convoy sailed in the clear dawn sunshine at six knots an hour – the best the holed tramp steamer could manage.

The ships kept a quarter of a mile apart from one another while a destroyer, HMS *Drake*, circled on submarine watch. They wended their way through minefields, guided by French pilots. There were alarms about U-boats, but only one appeared, and it was chased off by a depth charge.

At 11 a.m. on 18 June, a final flotilla of a dozen ships put to sea. The last to leave was a cargo vessel, the *Harpathian*. St-Nazaire was declared an open town to avoid fighting.

When news of the *Lancastria* disaster was brought to Churchill in the Cabinet Office, he immediately decided to suppress reports of what he called a 'frightful incident'. In his memoirs, he explained the decision as follows: 'I forbade its publication, saying, "The newspapers have got quite enough disaster for today at least." I had intended to release the news a few days later, but events crowded upon us so black and so quickly that I forgot to lift the ban, and it was some years before the knowledge of this horror became public.'[6]

On the other side of the war, William Joyce, 'Lord Haw-Haw', announced the sinking of the *Lancastria* in his broadcast that night. But the Nazi turncoat carried little credibility though, for once, he was telling the truth.

The news for Britain was, indeed, grim during those days in the middle of June. Italy's entry into the war on Germany's side raised a new threat in the Mediterranean and North Africa. Meeting Mussolini in Munich, Hitler talked of the impending invasion of Britain, though he was also reported to have told the Duce that he thought the British Empire represented 'an important factor in world equilibrium'. But, while he might harbour doubts about launching an offensive across the Channel and prefer to trust in the destructive power of the Luftwaffe, the Führer clearly envisaged reducing Britain to a subservient role while he ruled over a Nazi Fortress Europe.

The German advance in France remained remorseless. The Pétain government was pressing for an armistice, and nineteen National Assembly deputies who sailed to North Africa to continue the fight from there were promptly arrested. De Gaulle's historic broadcast from London declaring that France had lost a battle not the war made little impression across the Channel.

'What General Weygand called the Battle of France is over,' Churchill told the Commons on the afternoon of 18 June.

> I expect the Battle of Britain is about to begin. The whole fury and might of the enemy must very soon be turned on us. Hitler knows that he will have to break us in this island or lose the war. If we can stand up to him, all Europe may be free and the life of the world may move forward into broad, sunlit uplands. But if we fail, then the whole world, including the United States, including all that we have known and cared for, will sink into the abyss of a new Dark Age, made more sinister, and perhaps more protracted, by the lights of perverted science . . . Let us therefore brace ourselves to our duties and so bear ourselves that, if the British Empire and its Commonwealth last for a thousand years, men will still say 'This was their finest hour!'[7]

One of his prime concerns was to prevent France's fleet falling into German hands. It had been a theme the Prime Minister had repeated to the French during the previous week, and, despite seeking an armistice, the new government seemed to be of the same opinion.

The country's most modern warship, a still uncompleted battle cruiser called the *Jean Bart*, was in the construction yard at St-Nazaire. The French admiralty ordered her to sail for Morocco to keep out of German hands. The *Jean Bart*'s heavy guns had not yet been fitted, and her only defence was twelve machine guns, so she had to slip away before the Germans used their full aerial power against her. For their part, the British warned her commander, Captain Ronarc'h, that, if there was a risk of his ship falling into enemy hands, the Royal Navy and the RAF would attack her.

Crossing the course of the evacuation fleet, a destroyer, HMS *Vanquisher*, sailed to St-Nazaire with a vice admiral aboard to make sure that the French cruiser either left or was destroyed. An order was also sent from London to the *Highlander* to leave the convoy heading for home and to ensure the destruction of the *Jean Bart* if it did not put to sea. It was far from clear how this was to be achieved since it would have meant passing through two sets of lock gates or taking depth charges by hand along the quays. But dock workers and the crew of the *Jean Bart* got the ship out, and the men on the *Highlander* were greatly relieved when they received a second message saying the cruiser was making her way from port.

Not that her escape was a simple matter. When tugboats pulled the *Jean Bart* from the dock, the current floated her on to a sandbank. German planes launched bombing runs, hitting the deck. But the tugs pulled her free, and she made it to the open sea where she took fuel from a French tanker and steamed to North Africa.

*

St-Nazaire's pain was not over. On 19 June, German planes launched a major air raid on the town's centre, killing many people and destroying buildings along the main streets. Some locals blamed it on a group of Polish soldiers camped on a marsh outside St-Nazaire awaiting evacuation to England, who were said to have fired at a reconnaissance plane. Denise Petit of the Banque de France believed it was more of a reprisal for the way the British troops had escaped. Her own house was badly hit – not a single pane of glass was left in the windows, the balconies were torn off and the doors stood ajar. She and her mother left the town. Looters pillaged their home until a neighbour barricaded the entrance.

Some British soldiers were still in the town's hospitals, as the Wehrmacht soon discovered. An officer and two men marched in to the convent where George Youngs and ten other soldiers lay on mattresses on the floor. The officer told the British they were prisoners and must not try to escape. 'As long as you make no attempt to escape you will be cared for,' he promised. 'If you try to get away, you realise we can shoot you.'

The men were moved to a military hospital, Youngs clad in an outsized sports jacket and baggy trousers donated by a French civilian. At the new hospital, a nurse told them of a French coal ship that was trying to leave for England. There were no Germans around, and five of the British went to the quay.

Despite the intercession of locals urging him to take the soldiers on board, the captain of the collier refused to do so. People on the dock called him 'Pig, Boche, Traitor', but he insisted he would not sail with any foreign soldiers on board.

Anyway, he was heading for Algeria, not Britain. So the five returned to the hospital, where an English-speaking priest visited them with books and got Youngs a pair of spectacles to replace those he had lost when the *Lancastria* went down.

Some days later, through the big window of their ward, looking out at the sea, the wounded men saw a British destroyer passing by. Helped by the nurses, they got into a Red Cross ambulance standing outside the hospital and drove off in the direction the destroyer had taken. Fortunately for them, the Germans had not moved down that stretch of coast.

The ship, the *Punjabi*, was among six destroyers and seven transport ships sent to rescue the Poles, who were reported to number 8000. In fact, there were only 2000 and the size of the fleet was a considerable waste of resources: once again, the British commanders were operating on the basis of faulty intelligence.

Catching up with the destroyer, Youngs and his companions hailed her. The tall, bearded captain came in close to the shore, and asked them who they were.

They shouted that they were survivors of the *Lancastria*.

'How do I know that,' the captain asked

'You don't', they replied. 'You will either have to take a chance or leave us to the Jerries.'

A small boat was sent to fetch the soldiers. Brought to the captain's cabin to be questioned, they showed their British army papers. When they asked why he had decided to take them on, the captain said no German could have assumed Youngs' cockney accent.

CHAPTER 11

Home

THE FIRST RESCUE SHIPS entered Plymouth Sound and other harbours in south-west England on the afternoon of 18 June. Survivors remembered how beautiful the weather was, and their relief at reaching dry land. But some were struck by the apparent indifference of their compatriots to the threat of invasion. Gazing at the shore while his ship came in along the coast, Sergeant Harry Pettit was shocked to see the number of holidaymakers on the beaches. My God, he thought, they just do not know what is in store.

A Royal Marine band in full dress uniform played popular tunes to welcome the rescue boats. People sang along. The cheering was so loud that one officer remarked: 'You'd think we were winning this war, instead of losing it.'

On the *John Holt*, which had spent twenty-three hours on the voyage home, the captain took off his clothes for the first time in five days. Two weeks later, the boat set off without an escort to West Africa carrying 1090 French troops.

As the *Havelock* reached the Devonport naval base, Harry Pack of the RASC had a last look round to see if any of his friends were on board. He spotted Julie Delfosse, the Belgian woman he had swum with for four hours. After being picked up and put aboard a French trawler, she had found the son from whom she had been separated by the bombing of the *Lancastria*.

She told Pack she had been searching for him. 'She recognised me by my eyes,' he remembered. 'She wanted to thank me.'

With Church Army sisters acting as interpreters, Julie asked him for his home address. Harry was reluctant to give it, but she insisted, so he did. Then she went ashore to be reunited with her husband, and spend the rest of the war with him in Lancashire.

From the dockside, people threw packets of biscuits, tins of corned beef and tins of milk to the men on the ships. A flying tin of bully beef cut open the head of one soldier.

As the men came ashore, they were met by young women holding out trays of cigarettes. The Salvation Army and Church Army and Women's Voluntary Service distributed tea, sandwiches, fish and chips and postcards for men to write home that they were safe. The streets up from the docks were crowded with people, who emptied their pockets and handed over money, cigarettes and tobacco.

Some men arranged for telegrams to be dispatched to their homes saying they were still alive. In several cases, their parents had received messages from the authorities that their sons were missing in France, and were thought to have died. A chaplain sent a telegram to the parents of the *Lancastria* electrician, Frank Brogden, reporting that he had survived – they had previously been told he was thought to have been killed. When Joe Sweeney got home and rang the bell, his father turned pale as he opened the door: he and his wife had received a telegram from the War Office saying their son was missing in action and presumed dead.

The evacuated troops in best condition from the final episode of the evacuation of Operation Aerial went ashore first. Those from the *Lancastria* were kept till last; nobody wanted too many people to know what had happened.

Going down the gangplank, one man lost his balance after treading on the trailing edge of the blanket wrapped round a soldier in front of him. Two nurses grabbed him, and tried to lead him to a First World War ambulance with canvas sides. The more he resisted, the more convinced they were that he was suffering from shock. Eventually, he got away from them, and joined his comrades heading for a barracks building nearby.

On the quay, evacuees from the *Havelock* lined up to give three cheers for the destroyer's crew. The sailors cheered back. 'It was a moving moment,' Harry Pack recalled. 'Then we marched off – barefoot and filthy.'

Helpers lit cigarettes for men who were shaking so violently that they could not do so themselves. The badly wounded were carried into a fleet of ambulances, and given morphine.

While the wounded were treated in hospital, others were taken to naval barracks where they bathed and shaved. After that, they tucked into a huge meal of fish and chips washed down with mugs of tea. Some were directed to a school for deaf and dumb children. Members of the *Lancastria*'s crew went to the Seamen's Mission. The wireless truck driver, Leonard Forde, who had rowed out to a rescue ship, was billeted in a girls' school whose pupils had been hurriedly evacuated to make room for them. The men were amused to see a notice above an electric bell push reading: 'IF IN NEED OF A MISTRESS RING THIS BELL'!

Many survivors were bizarrely dressed in what clothes they had been able to get on the rescue ships. Some had only newspapers wrapped round them. Harry Pettit wore underpants and half a blanket. George Thomson, a 36-year-old NCO, walked ashore with two other survivors: none of them had any clothes. A woman relief worker asked if they would like a cup of tea. 'I'd rather have a pair of trousers,' Thomson replied. He was given a pair of sailor's bell bottoms, a Wasps rugby vest and a squadron leader's jacket.

As Joe Sweeney walked down the gangway, a big cheer went up and everybody started laughing. He looked round to see what was so funny, and then realised that it was the sight of him in the too-small clothes he had been given by the girl in the street in St-Nazaire and had ripped apart to accommodate his body. At the marine barracks, he was handed boots a size too small for him – they were the biggest available. It was seven months before he got a pair that fitted him, and he suffered in-growing toenails as a result.

Sergeant Major Picken was still in the pyjama bottoms and butcher's apron he had taken from a cupboard on a French trawler. He recorded being 'smuggled in' to Plymouth among columns of 'well uniformed chaps'. 'From our red, weathered faces, many people thought we were Gurkhas!' he added.

As Fred Coe shuffled along the street covered in a blanket, an 'extremely attractive' young woman approached him and led him to her home. There she gave him an Ever Ready single-blade safety razor, soap and a toothbrush while her mother provided soup and her father handed over clothes, including trousers that were six inches too short.

Captain Griggs went to a telephone box to call his family, who had not heard from him for more than a month. He told them that he was 'sound in wind and limb'. Then he used money in the wallet he had kept on him to buy new clothes.

After he had been issued with clothing, the one thing Bill Slater of the Pay Corps wanted was a beer. He had no British money, but he got ten francs from a friend, ordered a pint and handed over the French note. By the time the till was rung, he had drunk half the glass – and then he got tuppence change.

Sidney Dunmall paused at the quayside to fill up one of the letter cards to be sent to their families being handed out by the Salvation Army. 'I am well, am back in the UK,' he wrote. Then he got into a coach and was driven to a barracks where he and his colleagues feasted on roast beef and rice pudding before being taken on to Crown Hill Fort above Plymouth for a good night's sleep.

Jim Skeels had been given a smart uniform with gold braid by a marine gunner on the trip back from St-Nazaire. As the soldier walked down the gangplank at Plymouth, with his new uniform partly unbuttoned, two burly marines took him by the arms, lifted him off the ground and hustled him into a naval lock-up. An officer told him he had contravened regulations – 'A marine, even if he is dying, must have all buttons fastened.' Skeels got a message to his commanding major in the army who came and had him released, giving the marine officer a flea in his ear.

Denis Maloney, the sailor from the *Highlander* who had led the rescue of forty people in a lifeboat, also had trouble after landing. Initially, he and two mates were ignored when they arrived at Devonport, stinking and filthy with oil. They went to a barracks parade ground covered with people lying wherever they could. There, Maloney and his companions were each given an advance of five shillings against their pay.

Maloney went to a pub and drank a few pints of beer. When he came out into the street, he had gone only a hundred yards when he ran into a naval police patrol, who asked him where his gas mask was. They frogmarched him back to the barracks, and kept him under detention for the night. He expected to be court-martialled for leaving his ship without orders. Instead, the officers lined up to shake his hand. Later, however, an officer wrote on his papers, 'this man needs supervision'.

When the convoy that included the *City of Mobile* arrived in Plymouth, the men on board, who had been without food or water since leaving France, pushed aside the guards on a tender that came alongside with supplies. They grabbed the bread and ham, and set the water pump operating. Fred Hahn described them as 'thirst mad animals'. He, himself, went on to Southampton where he called his wife, Betty, from a telephone box.[1]

'Hallo, Fred,' she said. 'I knew you wouldn't drown. Have a lovely trip?'

'Lovely,' he replied. 'Sea as smooth as a mill pond and fine sunny weather. How's the kids?'

Another man on the *City of Mobile*, who had been irritatingly jittery on the voyage about submarines and mines, had a less welcoming reception when he telephoned home. According to Hahn, his father told him, 'you white-livered bastard. I hope I never see you again', and rang off.

A young woman, Muriel Hooper, of King Street in Plymouth, stood in the street with her autograph book, asking survivors to sign it.

'There will always be an England,' wrote one man from the RASC.

'Up and at 'em,' added another.

A sapper wished Miss Hooper, 'Good luck and all best wishes.'

Another man chose to draw a map of Holland.

Six decades later, Miss Hooper's autograph book lies among *Lancastria* memorabilia at the RAF station at Digby in Lincolnshire, home of the 73rd squadron which lost so many men on the liner.

When the Duggan family arrived in Plymouth from Brest on a cross-Channel steamer escorted by a minesweeper, they were held up for John's Bedlington terrier to be put into quarantine. That settled, Eddie Duggan went to try to get hotel rooms, but was turned away because he did not have enough English money. He rejoined the other civilians who had come over on the steamer, and they pooled their cash. Duggan took it to a big hotel where they got rooms at last.

Thirteen-year-old Emilie Legroux, who had been taken from a raft on to a rescue ship, was looked after in Plymouth by an Englishwoman from the Fairey Aviation branch there. Her mother and 11-year-old brother were housed in a refugee centre. Before long, Madame Legroux found her daughter, and the three of them tucked up in bed at a Salvation Army hostel. Later, they went to London and visited Trafalgar Square and Piccadilly Circus before settling in Hayes, Middlesex.

Isobella Macclaine Bowden, from Padstow in Cornwall, was working with the Red Cross in Plymouth when the survivors were brought ashore. She collected the letters they had written to say they were safe, and took them to the main post office which stayed open past midnight to handle the traffic. She also got home telephone numbers from some of those who had escaped the disaster, and placed calls during the night.

'I can't tell you who I am or where I am,' she said. 'But I have spoken to your husband (or boyfriend, father, brother). He's in England safe and sound and will be contacting you.'

In some cases, there was a silence at the other end of the line, and then a scream loud enough to wake the whole household, and a cry of 'He's home; he's safe.' Others just whispered, 'Thank you, thank you.'

Men who were taken to leave Plymouth by train were not told where they were heading; only the engine drivers knew that.

A detachment at the foot of the slope leading to the station looked so exhausted that it seemed they would not be able to stagger up with their rifles. A very young-looking lieutenant called them to attention, and gave the order to march. To cheers from onlookers, the men moved up the slope as though they were at their depots.

On the platform, a young soldier raced forward and grabbed a young woman from the Red Cross who was collecting letters from those boarding the train. He whooped with joy as he took her by the waist, swung her round and kissed her to a roar of laughter from the other soldiers. Then he politely apologised. He explained that, while leaving France, he had told himself that, if he got back to England, he would kiss the first pretty girl he saw.

There was a pleasant surprise at the station for Morris Lashbrook. Standing there when his unit assembled was his friend, 'Chippy' Moore, from whom he had been separated after they jumped together from the *Lancastria*.

In the evening, a dance was held with ladies from the WRAF; but most of the men just wanted to sleep, usually on the floor of military establishments in the town. Later, they remembered how wonderful it was to lie on a mattress with clean white sheets.

Others spent the night in pubs. In one, some of the *Highlander*'s crew met soldiers they had brought home, and they all made a night of it, singing and celebrating as they drank.

More decorously, in his new clothes, Captain Griggs had dinner at the house of the chief of the naval barracks where he stayed the night.

Barry Stevens, who had transferred from the *Havelock* to the *Highlander*, went to give a report to the commander in Devonport. Before he could do so, he passed out on the spot. Waking the next morning in a bed at Admiralty House, he was told by the commander that he obviously needed leave – he was given forty-eight hours.

In the main hospital, a young man lay in bed looking intently around him, but saying nothing. When the nurse, Isobella Macclaine Bowden, came round to collect outgoing mail from the patients and to wish them good night, the man in the next bed explained that his neighbour was Greek and spoke no English. The nurse clasped her hands and put them under her cheeks, closed her eyes and said, 'Sleep well.' When she opened her eyes, she saw the young man sitting up in bed, holding up one hand and pointing one finger. 'One sleep, no good,' he said. Then 'two sleep, ah' and he threw his arms round himself in a warm embrace.

Walking round a shed on the dockside, Harry Grattidge bumped into the Chief Engineer from the *Lancastria*, whom he had believed dead on the ship. Grattidge was still in the corporal's jacket and woollen underwear he had been given on the rescue ship. The engineer was clad only in an old patrol jacket. The two men pumped hands and, the Chief Officer recorded, 'grinned at one another like fools unable to speak'.[2]

On his return, Alan Brooke recorded that he 'thanked God for again allowing us to come home. I also thanked God that the expedition which I had hated from the start was over.'[3]

From the day he had arrived in France, he had seen that the battle on the continent had been lost, and that what mattered was to get as many men back to Britain as possible. Now what his biographer would describe as his 'vision . . . of a beaten France and of only Britain resurgent' had become reality.[4]

Brooke went to naval headquarters at Admiralty House in Plymouth, had tea, a bath and dinner – and took the midnight train to London, which was late arriving. At the War Office, he was questioned about why more equipment had not been brought back. His superiors seemed to have forgotten the order to save men and abandon or destroy material. Then Brooke went to his home in Hampshire to rest; six days later, he met Churchill for the first time over lunch and was appointed commander of the home front in preparation for the expected invasion from across the Channel – later, he would become Chief of the Imperial General Staff and chief military organiser of the British war effort.

The survivors who followed Brooke on the trains heading north from the coast during the following days were seen off at the station in Plymouth by women welfare volunteers handing out bags of soap, razor blades, sweets, cigarettes and matches. One group of survivors reciprocated with a singing concert including what were described as 'some rather rude songs'. As their train pulled out, they looked at the holiday crowds sunbathing on Dawlish beach, and contrasted what they saw with what they had been through.

When RAF Warrant Officer W. Horne got to London, the strange assortment of clothes he had been given on landing drew stares from other travellers on the Underground. Harry Grattidge set off for the capital by train in a second-hand suit with tuppence in his pocket. The Chief Officer's hair was still matted with oil, and the smell of fuel was on his breath. So strong was the odour that the other passengers in his compartment made for the refreshment car. At one point on the journey, an elderly man, who looked as though he was returning from holiday on the coast, beckoned him into the corridor, and said he could see he was in trouble. He offered Grattidge a pound to tide him over. The seaman said he did not need help; he was being met in London. The old man kept a close watch on him when they arrived to check the truth of his story.

Getting to Waterloo station, Sergeant Major Picken and some comrades were taken for escaped German prisoners, and detained in a waiting room. They were moved to Kensington Barracks, and held until the Sergeant Major, who had served there before, was recognised and allowed to telephone his wife, who had not heard from him for six weeks.

Taking a few days' leave in civilian clothes, Joe Sweeney found himself being shouted at by a woman who asked if he did not know there was a war on, and said he should be in the forces.

A Sherwood Forester who had donned an air force uniform while escaping from France was hauled in by military police, who asked him to which branch of the RAF he belonged. He said he was in the army. The police interrogated him as to why he was wearing an RAF uniform: in the end, he convinced them, and was released.

William Knight, who had driven across France in his lorry loaded with explosives, got back to Liverpool on a troopship after being picked up by a French fishing boat. When he was debriefed, he found that nobody wanted to know about the *Lancastria*, or to believe what he said. One of those who questioned him said he was suffering from a hallucination, and should be sent to an asylum.

Survivors were told that the sinking of the liner must be kept secret. It would be a breach of King's Regulations to say anything about what had happened at St-Nazaire. If the locals in Plymouth invited them to their homes, they were instructed by officers to refuse. In Liverpool, as the truth of what he was saying became evident, William Knight was told to keep quiet under the Official Secrets Act and to sign an undertaking not to mention what had taken place, particularly not to the press.

Reaching home in Faversham, Stan Flowers went to see the boss of a machinery works where he had been an apprentice before being called up. He told the older man that he had been in St-Nazaire, and had had a bit of trouble on a ship called the *Lancastria*. His ex-employer recalled that he had been on a cruise on her before the war.

Most of the survivors did not seem to have any desire to talk about the disaster, and wanted to put it behind them. Several who contributed recollections to the Lancastria Association more than half a century later had not previously talked about it, even to their wives and children. The soldiers and airmen were soon back in service, in Britain, Egypt and the Sudan or the Far East, and they did their best to push the tragedy to the back of their minds as they got on with the job of fighting the war. However, the experience would never dissolve. Later on, an airman who had been on the *Lancastria* jumped at a recruit who was singing 'Roll Out the Barrel' in a forces canteen and shouted at him to stop; then he apologised, saying, 'Sorry, chum. But we've got memories.'

Survivors were informed that they could ask to be reimbursed for personal losses of possessions, but then found their claims refused. The only thing for which payment was made was a Bible – whose value was put at twenty-five shillings. 'We resubmitted our claims, all claiming loss of Bible,' one

224 • *The Sinking of the Lancastria*

man recalled. 'We must have been a religious squad.' Captain Griggs put in for the total loss of all his kit, but some months later a suitcase was delivered to his home, having been picked up by the navy.

When Joe Sweeney and other survivors from his unit got back to their base in Nottinghamshire and went on parade, a brigadier stopped in front of them, and ordered that they should be put on a charge for having lost their rifles. Sweeney remonstrated, but the officer insisted. Fortunately, the brigadier left the base soon afterwards, and the matter was shelved. Another survivor was told off for the 'very serious offence indeed' of having lost his army identity disc.

Fred Hahn had a long slow train journey through blackouts to his regimental headquarters in Leicester, where he stayed in the Grand Hotel before being given forty-eight hours' leave. He headed for home at Cheadle Hulme, outside Manchester.

On the Saturday night, six days after the evacuation from St-Nazaire had started, he and his wife went to a dance at the Cricket and Tennis Club. As they arrived, the band was playing the Blue Danube waltz. A friend motioned to the musicians to stop playing while he greeted the survivor from France. As the music resumed, the Hahns began to waltz.

Back in France, 4000 troops were still left in St-Nazaire. Some were men saved from the *Lancastria* who had not been able to board the last rescue ships. Some got off on later rescue ships. Some were taken prisoner.

Others escaped, one group thanks to a 67-year-old retired

school teacher called Marie Rolland, who lived with her sister in the small town of Guémené-Penfao, north of Nantes. She formed one of the first Resistance networks, taking the codename of Annick. Her unit contacted survivors from the *Lancastria* still round St-Nazaire, and arranged for forty-seven of them to get back to England. Despite her age, she kept up an active career in the Resistance until the Gestapo identified her and put a price on her head, forcing her to go into hiding until 1944, when she was made a Companion of the Liberation, and decorated by Charles de Gaulle in person.

The loss of the *Lancastria* was felt particularly keenly in her home port; a quarter of the 330 crew had been lost. When the first survivors reached Liverpool by train, they found the station platform lined with women carrying photographs of their husbands, sons or boyfriends, asking if anybody had seen them. The wife of one sailor waited at Lime Street station for her husband, who she had been told had survived the disaster. He passed close to her as he left the train, but was so black with oil that she did not recognise him at first.

Captain Sharp and Chief Officer Grattidge met for lunch in a Liverpool pub to start work on a report on the disaster.

The Captain was puzzled as to why such a big ship with her bulkhead doors closed had sunk so quickly.

'My conclusion,' he wrote, 'is that each of the bombs which struck the ship passed through the upper deck and hatches, bursting in the ship and blowing holes in her sides. Then, apparently, a further bomb exploded in the water close to the side, just abaft the bridge, which probably added to the damage.'

The weather at the time, he added, 'was light NW wind, slight sea and swell, cloudy with bright periods'. The report, marked confidential, put the death toll at between 3000 and 4000, including seventy of the 330 crew.

As they lunched, Sharp told Grattidge that the two Belgian children with their dogs had not been picked up. The Chief Officer already knew that. In his memoirs, he recalled taking some comfort from the fact that their dogs had been with them to the end. 'I was still weak and light-headed with oil-poisoning,' he added. 'It seemed to me the best thing that had come out of it.'[5]

What he did not add was that, if he had not let the boy's look lead him to bend the regulations for the sake of humanity, the two children would not have boarded the liner, and could well have found a safe passage out of France on another boat.

Checking on survivors from his unit when they landed at Falmouth, the pince-nez-wearing accountant, Captain Clement Stott, was pleased to note that, apart from the two corporals and one sergeant who had died in the bombing, all his men had returned safely.

Then he headed home to Wales, wearing the ill-fitting uniform he had been supplied with along the way.

At the station, his wife put her arms around him, tears running down her cheeks.

'You know, Clem,' she said after a time, 'that battledress doesn't fit.'

His eyes wet, Stott replied: 'I know.'

'And you need a haircut,' his wife added.

So, on the way home, they stopped at the barber.

'Bit greasy your hair, Sir, isn't it?' he said.

'Yes,' the Captain responded. 'I've been in the water.'

Four days after the *Lancastria* went down, armistice talks between Germany and France opened in the Wagons Lits railway compartment where the surrender document had been signed at the end of the First World War. Hitler had ordered it to be pulled from a nearby museum to the place in the forest of Compiègne where the earlier capitulation had been formalised. The Führer, who had made a whirlwind tour of Paris beforehand, was present for the start of the negotiations. A monument commemorating the 1918 event was demolished after he had read its denunciation of the 'criminal pride of the German Empire' with a look said to combine hate, scorn, revenge and triumph.

A telephone line was opened to Bordeaux so that the government could follow the proceedings. On 22 June, the French agreed to the German conditions, and the country was divided between an occupied zone in the north and an unoccupied zone south of the Loire under the Pétain administration, which established itself in the spa town of Vichy. Churchill expressed 'grief and amazement' at the news. In London, Charles de Gaulle set up the Council of Liberation and the French National Committee declaring that, 'the war is not lost; the country is not dead; hope is not extinct; *Vive la France!*' But, for most of the French, it was time to stop fighting and for the refugees to go home – as the saying had it, in the summer of 1940, there were 40 million Pétainists.

The end of the debacle across the Channel had left the British, in the words of Churchill's military aide, 'Pug' Ismay, 'relieved, nay, exhilarated. Henceforth everything would be simpler; we were masters of our own fate.' The Prime Minister's private secretary, John Colville, found a line in Shakespeare's *Henry IV*: 'Tis better using France than trusting France.' At the Foreign Office, the senior civil servant, Sir Alexander Cadogan, confided to his diary: 'It will almost be a relief when we are left alone to fight the Devil, and win or die.'[6]

In the six weeks of fighting since 10 May, France had lost 90,000 dead, with another 200,000 wounded and as many as 2 million taken prisoner. A postscript to the Battle of France came when Britain's fear that the French fleet might eventually fall into Nazi hands led to a Royal Navy attack on ships at the Algerian port of Oran that destroyed two battleships and killed 1299 French sailors. German losses in the western offensive were put at 27,000 dead and 110,000 wounded. Casualties for the BEF were reported as 68,111 killed, wounded or missing.

By any estimate, the second evacuation of British troops from France in the early summer of 1940 was an enormous success. In the eight days after Alan Brooke landed at Cherbourg, 144,171 British soldiers and RAF personnel were taken off, plus 24,352 Poles, 18,246 French, 4,938 Czechs and 168 Belgians – making a total of 191,875, 57,175 of them from Nantes and St-Nazaire. Apart from the *Lancastria*, only two ships of any size were lost – the *Teresias*, sunk off St-Nazaire with no loss of life, and a troop carrier bombed during the movement of troops from Le Havre to Cherbourg. Fears of German submarines attacking the rescue ships proved unfounded. Though great quantities of equipment were left behind, some through the needless haste of the evacuation, 2292 vehicles, 1800 tons of stores and 310 guns were shipped back to Britain.

As the official historian of the war at sea, Captain Roskill, has remarked, in some ways it was 'an even more convincing demonstration of the effectiveness of sea power' than Dunkirk. But in a brilliant exercise in spin, which gave national morale an important boost, Churchill elevated the earlier evacuation to the status of a triumph in defeat. So it was best not to speak of those who had been left behind, and of what happened to the former Cunard liner in the bay off St-Nazaire. What is surprising is how this neglect persisted down the decades, cloaking Britain's worst maritime disaster in ignorance to this day.

CHAPTER 12

The Bodies

THE 15-YEAR-OLD FRENCH BOY was tending a potato patch on the sea marsh by the Bay of Noirmoutiers below St-Nazaire, at the end of June, when he saw the first bodies washing up on the beach. The tide on the bay goes out a long way, more than a mile. He and the other villagers of Les Moutiers-en-Retz had heard the explosions and bombing from up the coast in the middle of the month, but there had been no mention of the disaster at the time in the main regional newspaper. Later, another local newspaper, *Le Courrier de Pain-Boeuf*, had reported that a ship had been sunk, but gave no idea of how many lives had been lost.

In three weeks in late June and the first half of July, 128 bodies came ashore at Les Moutiers: one day, the tide brought in sixteen corpses. They were loaded on to carts drawn by oxen, and laid on straw in a mass grave at the top of the wide beach – the path there is still known as Chemin du *Lancastria*.

The Germans stripped the corpses of their papers and anything of value, and then called in Frenchmen to take them away for burial. In some places, a few locals went out to try to steal from the dead before the Germans reached them – the occupiers warned that anybody caught doing this would be deported.

The bodies on the wide beaches carried with them a collection of everyday objects: wristwatches, scissors, mirrors, rings, combs, pipes and tobacco pouches, whistles, cigarette cases, pencils, pens, penknives, bandages and purses. One man had put his false teeth in a pocket. There was the paraphernalia of military life – army paybooks, maps and identity discs – along with Bibles, rosaries and letters. The body of a 40-year-old soldier, which washed up on a jetty dressed in a cotton khaki shirt and blue trousers, had seventy francs in a pocket. Three men were identified from their driving licences, another by his cheque book from Barclays in Edgware Road, London.[1]

A 22-year-old had been carrying a letter written from the East Cliff Hotel in Cliftonville and a card inscribed 'Café Beth Marden, restaurant Citron House', plus two 100 franc notes. Another body had a letter on it from John Jaborn, 2, Clifton Street, Birmingham 18, and two ten shilling notes. There were cards from boarding houses, from a journalist on the *West London Observer*, and from a man in a town in the Loir et Cher department. On another corpse, a piece of paper was found with the address of Mlle Nadine Gossard, at an impasse in Abbeville. One man carried a medallion inscribed with the name of Lily and a cross of Lorraine.

On a fishing boat out at sea from the small port of Pornic, 18-year-old Claude Gourio noticed bloated bodies in the nets. There were a dozen in all. Gourio and the other fishermen on his boat put ropes round them to pull them back to their harbour. Some of the corpses were so decomposed that the arms came off on the way.[2]

In the following days, Gourio and the other fishermen came across big patches of oil in the sea, and found bodies floating in the middle of them. They brought the corpses back to land, and laid them out on the slipway in front of Pornic's casino before burying them. Five other bodies landed on the rocks along the coast outside the port. In mid-July, the local paper reported that hundreds of people strolling on the quayside watched a 'poor, blown-up body which, driven by strong westerly winds, was coming into the port on the galloping waves'. At the end of the jetty, a boat went to pull it to the shore where it was hoisted into the van of a local carpenter and driven away. A procession was held after evensong one Sunday evening in mid-July to bury the dead.

As summer drew on, more corpses were washed up all round the south of the bay, and down to the Île de Noirmoutier. Others were carried north to La Baule and surrounding ports. Swimming in the estuary, a French teenager felt his hand hit something. He turned to look. It was an arm floating in the sea. He carried it back to the shore, and put it on a rock.

Some bodies were swept out into the sea. A fisherman from the island of Yeu, where Marshal Pétain would be held after the war, found sixteen corpses tangled in his nets six months after the disaster – he took their identity discs and the papers in their wallets, kept them and handed them to a British naval ship that called in after the Liberation of France.

The tides swept other corpses and debris from the liner further down the west coast. A Frenchman found two wooden plates on the beach at Soulac-sur-Mer in the Médoc, 170 miles to the south. He could make out the lettering, in black paint, of the *Lancastria* on them. Since they would be considered as enemy materiel, he hid them in his attic until the end of the war when he sent them to England. Many years later, local fishermen still reported finding human bones in their nets, and presumed they came from the wreck in the estuary of the Loire.

The remains of Stan Flowers' friend from Faversham, Wally Smith, were washed nearly 100 miles south before coming ashore in salt marshes near the village of Triaize. The people who found the corpse buried it in secret, not telling the Mayor, who was a pro-Vichy collaborationist. After the war, Wally Smith was given a proper burial, but the locals did not know who he was. It was only in 1998 that the body was identified after the villagers heard a passing tourist speaking English in a restaurant, and took him to see their 'English body' in an unmarked grave. Wally was identified from the dog tags still on the body, and a commemoration was held the following year, attended by Stan Flowers and other survivors from the *Lancastria*.

The register of the Commonwealth War Graves Commission records 1816 of those who died on the *Lancastria*. More than four hundred bodies lie in cemeteries in western France. The largest is looked after by the Commission on a hill in Pornic, where the 266 graves include men from the Royal Engineers, Pioneer Corps, Royal Armoured Corps, Royal Artillery, Royal Army Service Corps, Royal Welch Fusiliers, Ordnance Corps, Cheshire regiment, Royal Hussars as well as the navy and air force, and a 60-year-old steward from the *Lancastria*.

The village cemetery in Les Moutiers has a special wall

dedicated to forty-six men interred there, from the Royal Engineers, Royal Welch Fusiliers, Royal Army Service Corps, the Buffs and Sherwood Foresters. Forty-three of the dead from the *Lancastria* are buried at the cemetery on a hill behind La Baule, among them a 19-year-old from the Argyll and Sutherland Highlanders, a 50-year-old from the Pioneer Corps, and men from the RAF, the Royal Army Service Corps, the Royal Engineers, the Royal Artillery and the Sherwood Foresters.

These bodies were reburied after the war. How they were treated at the time depended on the attitude of the German commanders in the occupied villages, and on the political sympathies of local mayors. Some refused to allow burial in cemeteries, so the corpses were put in trenches dug at the top of the beaches. At Clion-sur-Mer, on the other hand, the Mayor had trees cut down to make coffins.

In the coastal village of La Bernerie, 120 bodies were taken in coffins on carts from the sea front to the stone and concrete church, accompanied by a German guard of honour and a detachment of soldiers carrying a wreath. A crowd of local people and officials gathered, and absolution was sung while the bells tolled. The coffins were then lowered into a trench grave. A triple gun salute was fired. The senior German officer present said the soldiers who had just been buried 'fought for their country with the same courage as we did for ours and our Führer'.

CHAPTER 13

————

Aftermath

TWO DAYS AFTER THE DISASTER in St-Nazaire, a correspondent of *The Times* on the south-west coast of England wrote an account of what had happened, reporting that there had been about 5000 people on board the *Lancastria* – and that around half of them had been saved. The story told of a major who had 'a miraculous escape' when a bomb dropped through his cabin, of a lieutenant who had been standing on deck within a few feet of the first bomb but got out unscathed, and of civilians who swam to safety. Because of Churchill's imposition of censorship, the story was not printed.

Telegrams from the military authorities to the families of those who had been on board the liner said simply that the men were missing in action, without giving any details of where they had been lost. So their relatives thought they had died in the Battle of France: Wally Smith's parents were told he had perished at Dunkirk.

Finally, the news of the disaster appeared, not in Britain but across the Atlantic after the New York *Sun* got hold of the photographs taken by Frank Clements on the *Highlander,* and broke the story on 25 July. British correspondents promptly picked up the news, and cabled it to London where *The Times* ran a story quoting the New York paper. On 26 July the Ministry of Information announced the loss of the liner, and the press and the BBC finally reported what had happened at St-Nazaire more than five weeks earlier.

'Troopship lost – Bombed in BEF evacuation – Heavy casualties,' read the headline above the story by the aeronautical correspondent of *The Times,* which put casualties at about 2500 – one of the dead, it said, was a padre of an RAF squadron who had refused to leave St-Nazaire on a earlier boat because he did not want to abandon a crate full of Bibles.[1] The dispatch from the local reporter which had been held since 19 June was printed below.

The *Daily Mirror* splashed with the story and a photograph of the liner going down. It put the death toll at 2823. The *Daily Telegraph* estimated the number on board at 5350, of whom nearly 2500 were known to have been saved. 'It is thought that others may have made their way ashore and fallen into enemy hands,' the paper added.

The *Illustrated London News* ran a picture spread at the beginning of August headlined: 'When a Troopship founders: The ordeal of "*Lancastria*" survivors'. The magazine, *War Illustrated,* followed with a feature showing photographs Clements had taken of bedraggled survivors crowding on to the *Highlander.* The headline read: 'Men of the "*Lancastria*" Gritted Their Teeth and Smiled at Death'.

After that flurry of attention, the story disappeared. At most, Britain's worst single maritime disaster was reduced to

a passing reference in the history of the Second World War.
A report by the Commander-in-Chief of Western Approaches
to the War Office on the war at sea, dated 5 August, simply
noted: 'the behaviour of the troops and crew of S.S.
LANCASTRIA under most trying circumstances was beyond
all praise'.[2]

The authorities classified most of the dead as 'Missing'
since their deaths could not be confirmed, and there was a
faint hope that they had got ashore and were prisoners of war.
When the families sought news, officials could give none. The
records of some military units had gone down with the ship.

Joe Sweeney travelled up to Hexham in Northumberland
to console the mother of a man from his unit who had died
on the liner. The woman ran a small grocer's shop just behind
the church. She wept for an hour, occasionally whimpering,
'I lost my husband in the First World War and now my only
son.' It was, Sweeney recalled, the most poignant experience
of his life.

The anguish of mothers and wives is evident from their
letters kept in War Office files.[3] In November 1940, a Mrs
Sapsford of Teddington, whose son had been on the
Lancastria, wrote: 'I had been building such hopes of him
having been picked up . . . It's a terrible bit of dirty business
altogether, our dear Lads should be homeward bound. I'm
speaking for all mothers, poor souls, 21 years to have their
lives cut off, for the sake of being held up for a few minutes
& already overloaded.'

Mrs Sapsford added that she had received a visit one
Sunday afternoon from an unidentified man who said his son
had been a great friend of her boy. He added that 'he had
applied at the right quarters, and [been told] that his Son
Ken . . . went down to get a meal when the bomb went off,

why werent we informed from you to that effect, instead of him coming to tell us. I think that needs an explanation. Unfortunately, I don't know his Surname or address only that he came from Southall.'

Isabel West of Kingston upon Thames wrote to the War Office to say that she had spoken to a man who saw her son on the liner – 'he was going up the stairway as my son was going down, he spoke to him for a while, my son would have just got below when the ship was struck, he did not see him again. That is all I have been able to find out. I have no further news. I wish I had, it is a great sorrow to us, my son was a fine boy.'

'I am on the point of a Breakdown and my dear baby is in very bad health,' wrote Mrs D. Hamper of Hove, whose husband had been a sapper. 'Oh if you could give me some news! If you have bad news for me I would rather know as I know God will give me strength to bear this trouble. I do ask kindly if you will try & give me definite news & let me know what has happened to my dear husband. Do write to me soon.'

There was nothing the authorities could say in response. They had little idea who had perished on the *Lancastria*, or whether men who had not been brought back to Britain were still alive as prisoners.

On 25 June, the Cabinet War Room Report noted: 'The armistice between France and Germany came into effect at 0035 hours BST today when hostilities ceased. The Bordeaux Government signed an armistice with Italy at 1815 hours BST on 24th June. There is nothing further of importance to record on this front.'[4]

The evacuation was not quite finished, however. There

were still 2500 French and British troops left on Ouessant Island off the north-west coast of France. They were shipped to Britain in the following weeks, before a German naval party took possession of the island.

On 20 July, the War Cabinet was told that 16,000 men had surrendered or were missing in France. Among them were those who died on the *Lancastria*, though the official reports made no mention of them.

St-Nazaire went on to have a rough war. The day after the French signed the armistice with Germany, British planes launched their first raid on the port. The harbour facilities were important berths for German battleships while its submarine pens were strategically placed for U-boats in the Battle of the Atlantic. These made it a prime target, so air attacks continued for the rest of the war.

In March 1942, British commandos landed to try to knock out the submarine bases, sailing in over the wreck of the *Lancastria*. Crossing the flatland by the sea, one of the officers looked back at the estuary and saw the liner's masts poking out of the water at low tide. The raid put a big dry dock out of commission, but most of the attackers were killed.

An Allied air assault in early 1943 destroyed 60 per cent of the houses in the town, and made another 20 per cent uninhabitable. Visiting St-Nazaire, the German naval commander, Admiral Dönitz, remarked that there was 'not a cat, nor a dog left; nothing left except for the submarine shelters'. Later, German troops in the St-Nazaire pocket were among the last to hold out. When the war ended, only 100 of the original 8000 houses in the town were standing.

*

On 8 October 1940, the *London Gazette* announced the award of OBEs to Captain Sharp, Harry Grattidge and the *Lancastria*'s chief engineer, James Dunbar. Three other crew members were also decorated, as were three men from the *Cambridgeshire*, though an administrative mix-up meant that this did not take place until 1942.

Grattidge, who was due £50 from Cunard in compensation for his possessions and clothes lost on the *Lancastria*, felt the pain of the disaster for weeks. 'A seaman is cut to the heart when an accident befalls his ship,' he wrote.[5] 'But something dies inside him for ever if he loses her.'

The Chief Officer dreamed of the brooding silence before the bombs hit. When he woke, he would be trembling and sweating, though he felt cold at the same time. He went to his home town of Stafford, and tried to forget his experience in a round of parties. Then a cousin took him to a house where he cut himself off from the world in his bedroom. After three days, Harry found he could sleep properly once more, though he remained a little deaf as a result of the explosions.

He went back to work as an officer on a ship carrying planes from the United States to Britain. Surviving the war, he rose to become Chief Captain of the Cunard line and Captain of the *Queen Mary*.

Rudolph Sharp, whose compensation as a captain amounted to £100, was not so fortunate. In 1941, he was put in charge of the *Lanconia*, another Cunard liner which had been turned into a troopship. One voyage took her to South Africa – also on board for the outward voyage was another *Lancastria* survivor, Harry Pack of the RASC.

On the way back to Britain, the ship was torpedoed by a German submarine. Sharp stayed on board as she sank, with the First Officer, George Steel. As the last men left on the final lifeboat, Sharp asked them for a cigarette, and they saw its glow as they pulled away. The death toll of 1614 on the *Laconia* was the second worst of any single boat in the war, after the *Lancastria.*

Among the other boats that took men from St-Nazaire, the *John Holt* was sunk by a submarine off Africa. The *City of Mobile* was bombed and went under while plying from Glasgow to Liverpool. The KG30 Luftwaffe wing took part in the Battle of Britain. Peter Stahl was awarded the German Gold Cross in 1942 for his war services.

CHAPTER 14

The Memory

ON A RAINY JUNE AFTERNOON, *Lancastria* survivors, Fred Coe, Alec Cuthbert, Stan Flowers, Harry Harding, Bob Peterson and Morris Lashbrook, take their places in the pews of St Katharine Cree Church in the City of London for the annual memorial service for those who died in the Loire estuary in 1940. In the front row sits Denis Maloney, who helped to haul forty men from the water into a lifeboat from the *Highlander*. Round them are fifty relatives and members of the *Lancastria* Association, some wearing blazers or scarves emblazoned with a badge with the date of 17 June 1940 picked out in gold.

They listen as officers of the Association report that Gaston Noblanc, the French boy who had thrown himself into the rescue effort, joined the Resistance and had been tortured by the Germans, is very seriously ill. Flowers have been sent to his wife, who has telephoned her thanks.

Fred Coe leaves his pew and goes to the rear of the church. Straight-backed in a dark suit, white gloves and a beret, he carries the standard of the *Lancastria* Association on a long wooden staff down the aisle. The banner is blue and black with the name of the liner in gold. When Coe reaches the altar steps, the Association's chaplain takes the banner from him, and places it against the wall. Fred goes to sit in the front row, beside Denis Maloney, who had been in charge of the boat that saved him sixty-four years before.

To their right, a panel in a stained-glass window commemorates the *Lancastria*, showing a lifeboat pulling away from the stricken ship below an image of Christ walking on the water. The words on a brass plaque declare: 'TO THE GLORY OF GOD AND IN PROUD MEMORY OF MORE THAN 4,000 PEOPLE WHO DIED WITH THE TROOPSHIP *LANCASTRIA* AND TO HONOUR ALL WHO TOOK PART IN THE WORK OF RESCUE', followed by a list of the eighteen British rescue ships and the French fishing boat, the *Saint-Michel*, on which Joan Rodes crossed the bay on 17 June.

After the first hymn – 'Guide Me, O Thou Great Redeemer' – led by a ten-strong choir, the chaplain offers a prayer in memory of those who died or were injured off St-Nazaire. 'Their example has encouraged us, their witness has inspired us and the memory of them makes us glad this day,' the prayer goes. 'For them all we thank Thee, we honour Thee and we worship Thee, as they do now by your grace and in your glory.'

The choir sings Psalm 46, followed by a reading from Ecclesiasties by the Association's Chairman, noting the glory earned by humble as well as famous men. The chaplain prays for those who sail the sea, also mentioning Gaston Noblanc by name. The sermon, given by a priest from another church in the City, speaks of the old fear of the sea as a dangerous place, and the way in which safety can be achieved by faith in God.

After the last hymn has been sung, Fred Coe leaves his pew, adjusts the leather harness round his neck and shoulder, and goes back to the altar steps. Three survivors accompany the priest in the blessing of a painting of the *Lancastria* in peace-time. A wreath is laid.

Coe lowers the tip of the standard till the banner unfurls on the floor as an army trumpeter sounds the Last Post. The congregation stands in silence, the only sounds coming from the rain on the window and a ticking clock at the back of the knave. Then the trumpeter blows Reveille, and Coe lifts the standard back to the vertical position.

The 'Marseillaise' is sung, the choir intoning the French words as strongly as if it was their own anthem. Then comes 'God Save the Queen', after which the chaplain offers a final prayer: 'Lord support us all the day long of this troublous life. Till the shades lengthen, the evening comes, the busy world is hushed, the fever of life is over and our work is done; then Lord in thy mercy, grant us safe lodging, a holy rest and peace at the last, through Jesus Christ, our Lord, Amen.'

The survivors gather at the altar for a group photograph. Then they go into a side room with relatives of those who were on board the liner for sandwiches, cakes and tea.

Denis Maloney recounts how he went straight on from the rescue at St-Nazaire to serve on ships hunting U-boats in the Atlantic and on commando raids in the Middle East before sailing to China where he saw the Communist victory over the Nationalists in 1949.

Stan Flowers tells how the wallet he lost when he shed his trousers in the sea was found and returned to him in 1950; it must have been washed ashore quickly because he could still read the concert party programme tucked inside.

Alec Cuthbert, his eyes twinkling, recalls how he floated in the water for three hours with a man he did not know hanging on to his life jacket. Fred Coe says he did not dwell on the disaster after getting back to England because 'life goes on'.

Coincidences bring survivors together. Two met in the gentlemen's toilet of the Savoy Hotel while attending a marriage there. When Harry Pettit opened his garden for charity, a visitor recognised a photograph of the *Havelock* in his bungalow – he turned out to be the man who, as a 19-year-old, had fished Harry from the water on to a rescue raft.

Returning from a trip to Australia by sea, Morris Lashbrook fell into conversation with a woman who was coming to Europe. She said one object of her trip was to visit St-Nazaire. Her husband had been among the RAF men who had died on 17 June. She asked Morris if he knew about the disaster. He told her the story of what had happened; she was very grateful as all she knew was from an Air Ministry telegram telling her that her husband was missing.

The *Lancastria* Association has 300 members, most of them relatives of those who were on board on 17 June 1940, and wish to honour their memory – or celebrate their survival. Established in 1980, it is the second such organisation, succeeding an earlier one set up after the war. Around 100 survivors are thought to be alive, some in Australia, New Zealand, Africa and North America. On Remembrance Sunday, a group of a dozen men from the Association joins the march past the Cenotaph. Regional get-togethers are held.

An annual service is also organised at the National Memorial Arboretum in Alrewas, Staffordshire, where a plot is dedicated to the liner and its dead.

Survivors visit the graves of those who died on the liner. In 1990, Harry Pettit walked through the cemetery at La Baule and saw a stone with no name but S147653 engraved on it. He recognised it as the service number of a friend with whom he had jumped from the *Lancastria* fifty years earlier.

Former sapper Norman Driver went back to the forest where he and his Royal Engineers unit had been building a railway line when they were told to head off for St-Nazaire. The dirt track they had used had been tarred, and new bungalows had been built. He asked about the farmer's son who had sat and watched the soldiers at work – Norman had always regretted having been marched off from the forest without having had time to say goodbye to the boy.

A house was pointed out to him. When a man opened the door, Driver said, 'Monsieur Couedel?' The man replied 'Oui.' Driver told him who he was. In English, the Frenchman replied: 'You dead! You dead!'

Driver explained how he had survived the sinking of the *Lancastria*. When he left, Laurent Couedel presented him with two bottles of wine and a chisel he had found from the Royal Engineers workshop.

In the summer of 2000, two dozen members of the *Lancastria* Association undertook a sixtieth anniversary pilgrimage to the site of the disaster, sailing out to the orange buoy which floats above the liner's last resting place, with her name spelled out on its metal superstructure. Michael Sheehan, the Canadian helmsman from 1940, cast the first wreath of red poppies on to the sea. A piper played a lament. A soldier recited a prayer starting, 'There are no roses on a sailor's grave; Nor wreaths upon the storm-tossed waves.' As the survivors paid their respects to the dead, a dolphin suddenly jumped out of the sea, executed a turn and swam away.

Below them, undisturbed by anything but the tides, lay the wreck of the liner from which they had escaped sixty years earlier. The once-proud Cunarder is seventy-two feet down on the seabed. Ships travelling in the estuary steer clear of her, using the buoy as a navigation aid.

Strong currents make diving dangerous, so the *Lancastria* has been undisturbed. One diver who went down after the war was said to have reported glimpsing skulls behind the portholes, but some local people think that was a matter of poetic licence. Another who dived in 2000 said the water was so dirty that he could not see anything. As the tide changes, the water around the wreck grows cloudy from the mud and debris on the seabed, and a dark stream rises towards the surface.

The *Lancastria* has been designated a maritime monument by the French, meaning that it cannot be moved or interfered with. In St-Nazaire, a stone memorial on the seafront looks out at the site of the wreck, dedicated to 'more than 4,000 who died'.

Why the loss of the *Lancastria* remained so little known for more than six decades is a mystery, but, in the context of the summer of 1940, the silence said much about the national mood. After Dunkirk, the battle for Britain was looming, with a German invasion force poised across the Channel. The country seemed to sense the need to keep morale high in the face of the all-conquering enemy who encapsulated evil. Nobody wanted to hear of a disaster in which thousands of defenceless people died, or to be told that Dunkirk had not drawn the final line under the retreat from France. There was no desire to be told that 150,000 men had been left behind, most of them not dashing fighters of the kind who would fly in the Battle of Britain but the ordinary support troops who keep an army going – repair workers, carpenters, communications staff, ground crews, bakers and cooks and NAAFI store men.

Unlike Dunkirk, which was converted in the British imagination from a desperate retreat into a monument to the national spirit, the afternoon of 17 June in St-Nazaire could not be turned from defeat into a semblance of victory. Lying helpless in the estuary as the Luftwaffe swooped, the liner could all too easily have become a symbol for the island that was about to be pummelled from the air. For all their valour and defiance, the men singing 'There'll Always Be an England' had been powerless to ward off disaster.

The fate of those who died on the *Lancastria* or in the oily sea, and of those who survived, was a human story, not a military one – and many of those who got away preferred to move on to other things as soon as they could. They did not dwell on what had happened, but joined their units to continue the war against Hitler. As Fred Coe said, 'Life goes on.'

Still, at the lowest estimate, 2500 people died that day. An Admiralty report said 2823 had been lost, and Churchill wrote of a toll of 'upwards of 3,000 men'. Both figures may well be underestimates given that several reports set the number on board at more than 6000, and those saved were put at 2500.

If that sounds high, another liner took 6000 off from Brest during the Operation Aerial evacuation, and some survivors from the *Lancastria* have talked of as many as 8000–9000 having been on board.

Whatever the estimate, the loss of the liner was the worst maritime disaster to a single ship in British history, even if it was relegated to a footnote in the impending battle for national survival. The size of the death toll was all the more shocking because it could so easily have been much lower, or perhaps avoided altogether.

The *Lancastria* was the only big ship hit in the second evacuation from France. If embarkation had stopped when 5,000 had come aboard, the dead would have been significantly fewer. One or two thousand soldiers and RAF men might have been taken to another of the rescue ships in the estuary. If those caught in the holds had not been sent below for safety, their chances of escape would have been much greater. The amount of oil in the tanks increased the choking slick that spread out from the dying ship. The failure to tell men how to enter the water if they were wearing a life jacket resulted in many broken necks. Had Captain Sharp had followed the instructions from the naval commander, the liner would have been at sea when the Junkers swooped. He was worried about submarines, but none of the other ships returning to England from St-Nazaire was attacked by a U-boat.

That collection of 'ifs' may make the tragedy an example of how an accumulation of factors can come together to cause a disaster, but the heroism and fortitude shown by those who found themselves in the water as the liner went down reflects the spirit of 1940. Some gave in to despair, yet the overriding image is one of men, and the few women who were on board, refusing to succumb. Evocations of stiff upper lips have become unfashionable, but this was what was in evidence that June day, from the men standing on the hull singing patriotic songs to the people refusing to abandon hope in the sea. With breathtaking suddenness, four bombs had turned pleasure at having reached such a fine, solid ship into the worst experience of their lives. Whether helping one another in the sea or singing on the sinking hull, they reacted in a way hard to imagine today.

If only for that, the plaque by the seafront in St-Nazaire proclaims: 'We have not forgotten.'

NOTES

Prologue

1. Churchill, *The Second World War*, Vol. 2, p. 194
2. Ibid., p. 194

Chapter 1: Friday, 14 June 1940

1. Grattidge, *Captain of the Queens*, p. 150
2. Horne, *To Lose a Battle*, pp. 519–23
3. Cadogan, *Diaries*, 2 June 1940
4. Booth, *European Spring*, p. 293
5. Cadogan, *Diaries*, 2 June 1940
6. Spears, *Assignment to Catastrophe*, pp. 138–59
7. For account of Briare see Spears, pp. 138–59; Jenkins, *Churchill*, pp. 613–616; Reynaud, *In the Thick of the Fight*, pp. 483–9
8. Defence Committee, London, 8 June 1940: Jenkins, p. 611; Spears, p. 149

9. Churchill, p. 162

10. Cadogan, *Diaries*, 2 June 1940

11. For account of Tours, see Spears, pp. 198–220; Cadogan, *Diaries*, 13 June 1940; Jenkins, pp. 617–18; Churchill, pp. 157–67

12. CAB 65/7

13. Jackson, *The Fall of France*, p. 97

14. Karslake, *1940, The Last Act*, pp. 262–3. Karslake's report on pp. 253–3 summarises his view of the debacle and French policy towards British forces.

15. Karslake, Appendix A, lists units

16. Ibid., pp. 179–82; PREM3/188/5 at Public Records Office, Kew (PRO)

17. Ibid., pp. 156 et seq; PREM3/188/5 p. 80 at PRO

18. Mervyn Llewelyn-Jones' diary, 9–14 June 1940

19. War Office (WO) 167/117 at PRO

20. Brooke, *War Diaries*, p. 74

21. Ibid., p. 80

22. Ibid., p. 81–82

Chapter 2: Saturday, 15 June 1940

1. Llewelyn-Jones' diary, 15 June 1940

2. Grattidge, *Captain of the Queens*, p. 152

3. Spears provides an acid, and probably accurate, portrait of her.

4. Brooke, *War Diaries*, pp. 83–6

5. Naval report, ADM 199/371 at PRO

6. Roskill, *War at Sea*, p. 239

7. Ibid., p. 236

8. Colville, *The Fringes of Power*, p. 158

Chapter 3: Sunday, 16 June 1940

1. Colville, *The Fringes of Power*, p. 158
2. Ibid., p. 159–60
3. Ibid., p. 159–61; Horne, *To Lose a Battle*, p. 659
4. *Courrier de St-Nazaire et de la Région*, 6–13 July 1940
5. Denise Petit's diary, p. 12
6. Stahl, *The Diving Eagle*, p. 53
7. *The Times*, 18 June 1940
8. Spears, *Assignment to Catastrophe*, p. 293
9. Ibid.
10. WO 167/918 at PRO
11. Spears, pp. 316–17
12. Colville, pp. 163–5
13. WO 167/117 at PRO
14. Ibid.
15. Ibid.

Chapter 4: Monday, 17 June 1940

1. Grattidge, *Captain of the Queens*, pp. 152–3
2. Denise Petit's diary
3. WO 167/1155 at PRO
4. Brooke, *War Diaries*, p. 86

Chapter 5: The Bombing

1. Grattidge, *Captain of the Queens*, p. 107
2. Ibid., p. 155
3. Barry Stevens' diary
4. Churchill speech, Hansard, Vol. 362, columns 51–61
5. Stahl, *The Diving Eagle*, p. 40

6. Grattidge, pp. 153–4

Chapter 6: The Sinking

1. Stahl, *The Diving Eagle*, pp. 54–5
2. WO 167/1155 at PRO
3. Stahl, p. 55

Chapter 7: The Sea

1. Captain Sharp's report, ADM 199/2133 at PRO

Chapter 8: The Rescue

1. ADM 1/12264 at PRO
2. Bond, *Lancastria*, pp. 223–6
3. Grattidge, *Captain of the Queens*, p. 159
4. Ibid.

Chapter 9: St-Nazaire

1. Fred Hahn's papers, Imperial War Museum
2. Ibid.

Chapter 10: The Way Back

1. Admin 199/76, WH 7063 case at PRO
2. Brooke, *War Diaries*, p. 86
3. Ibid., 87–8
4. 'Life and Times of Captain Barry Kenyon Stevens' by Admiral Guy F. Liardet, February 1996, private paper in author's possession.

5. Fred Hahn's papers, Imperial War Museum
6. Churchill, *The Second World War*, Vol. 2, p. 172
7. Ibid., pp. 198–9

Chapter 11: Home

1. Fred Hahn's papers, Imperial War Museum
2. Grattidge, *Captain of the Queens*, p. 160
3. Brooke, *War Diaries*, p. 88
4. Bryant, *The Turn of the Tide*, pp. 180–6 on Brooke's return.
5. Grattidge, p. 161
6. Cadogan, *Diaries*, 17 June 1940
7. Roskill, *The Navy at War*, p. 81

Chapter 12: The Bodies

1. This and next paragraph, WO 32/18802 at PRO
2. Gurio, interview with author

Chapter 13: Aftermath

1. *The Times*, 26 July 1940
2. Admin 199/76 WH case 7063 at PRO
3. WO 32/18802 at PRO
4. CAB 100 at PRO
5. Grattidge, *Captain of the Queens*, p. 161

BIBLIOGRAPHY

Accounts by survivors of their time in France, of the sinking of the *Lancastria* and of their subsequent journey back to Britain, have been taken from interviews by the author, oral history tapes at the Imperial War Museum and, above all, from two collections of narratives: *The Loss of the Lancastria*, compiled by John L. West and published by Millgate Publishing; and *HMS Lancastria: Narratives*, compiled and published by the Lancastria Survivors Association. Official War diaries and War Office documents are from the Public Records Office at Kew, the Imperial War Museum, and RAF records of 73rd Squadron at RAF Digby, Lincolnshire. The diary of Mervyn Llewelyn-Jones and the typescript of Fred Hahn's account are at the Imperial War Museum. Captain Sharp's reprort is at the PRO – ADM 199/2133. The Hirst family website at http://groups.msn.com/HirstFamilyWebsite/ homepage2.msnw has a wealth of detail about the liner and the disaster. The eventual publication of news of the sinking is taken from newspapers of

26 July 1940, at the Newspaper Library, Colindale. The evidence from Barry Stevens comes from his unpublished diary in the possession of the author. French naval documents mentioned in the text are from the naval archives at Vincennes. Local French documents, including Denise Petit's account and contemporary newspapers, are in the departmental archives in Nantes and the Eco-musée in St-Nazaire. Memoirs, diaries and other works used as sources are as follows:

Alanbrooke, Field Marshal Lord, (ed. Alex Danchev and Daniel Todman) *War Diaries, 1939–1945*, (London: Weidenfeld & Nicolson, 2001)

Bryant, Arthur, *The Turn of the Tide, 1939–43* (London: Collins, 1959)

Bond, Geoffrey, *Lancastria* (London: Olbourne, 1959)

Booth, Clare, *European Spring* (London: Hamish Hamilton, 1941)

Bourdon, Emile, *L'Inattendu* (Laval: Siloë, 1996)

Cadogan, Sir Alexander, (ed. David Dilks) *The Diaries of Sir Alexander Cadogan, O. M., 1938–1945*, (London: Cassell, 1971)

Colville, John, *The Fringes of Power* (London: Hodder & Stoughton 1985)

Churchill, Winston, *The Second World War,* Vol. 2 (London: Cassell, 1950)

Flowers, Vic, *Premonition of Disaster* (Wartime News, 1998)

Grattidge, Harry, *Captain of the Queens* (London: Olbourne, 1956)

Gilbert, Martin, *Second World War* (London: Weidenfeld & Nicolson, 1989)

Horne, Alistair, *To Lose a Battle: France, 1940* (London: Penguin, 1979)

Jackson, Julian, *The Fall of France* (Oxford: OUP, 2003)

Jenkins, Roy, *Churchill* (London: Pan, 2002)

Karslake, Basil, *1940, The Last Act* (London: Leo Cooper, 1979)

Kersaudy, François, *De Gaulle et Churchill* (Paris: Perrin, 2001)

Maclean, Alistair, *The Lonely Sea* (London: Collins, 1985)

Reynaud, Paul, *In the Thick of the Fight* (London: Cassell, 1955)

Roskill, S.W., *War at Sea* (London: HMSO, 1954)

——, *The Navy at War* (London: Collins, 1960)

Stahl, Peter, *The Diving Eagle* (London: William Kimber, 1978)

Spears, Edward, *Assignment to Catastrophe*, Vol. 2 (London: Heinemann, 1954)

Williams, Charles, *The Last Great Frenchman* (London: Little Brown, 1993)

Winter, John de S, *BEF Ships Before, At and After Dunkirk* (Gravesend: World Ship Society, 1999)

INDEX